Spark!

Spark!

10 secrets to living the life you love

Doug Mendenhall

Spirit Press
Portland, Oregon
www.spiritpress.org

ISBN 1-893075-54-3

Cover Art and Design by Chad Harder
Book Design by Spirit Press
Editing by Linda Meyer and Tim Healea

Spirit Press
www.spiritpress.org
PO Box 12346
Portland, Oregon 97212

Dedication

This book is dedicated to everyone who wants to live a life full of passion, enthusiasm, love, warmth, and absolute joy. I hope this book will provide a process to increase your level of spark in the world!

Acknowledgements

Spark has taken over three years to create, including two years of research. It took the input and combined talents of over one hundred and twenty people and has been a truly passionate project. I especially wish to thank and acknowledge the following people:

First and foremost, those who shared their insights, wisdom, and lessons on how to keep Spark: Cathy Hawk, John Chapman, Dr. José Zaglul, Chuck Collins, Fran Korten, Susan Clark, Mickey Connolly, Laura Stepp, Terri Watson, Lori Wisbeck, Gary Hirsch, Kathy Longholland, Kasey Mahaffy, Mechai Vivavaidya, Mary Jo (MJ) McConnell, Scott Newman, Tammy Gilley, Tricia Brennan, Frank Fredregill, Heidi Henzel, Tamra Fleming, Darcy Winslow, Lindsay Andreotti, Steve Knaebel, Aaron Hornstein, Rick Durden, Joe Zaniker, Linda Devers, Martin Goebel, Jelly Helm, Lorenzo Rosenzweig, Alberto Saavedra, Enrique Penalosa, Shari Black, Emily Gates, Trung Tu, Jerry Porras, Pat Breslin, Tom Linebarger, Joe Hughey, James Polsfut, Jack Vaughn, Anna Scott, Scott Dawson, Simon Bailey, Kay Stepp, Colleen Kelly, Bill Gates, Sr.,, and Maggie Kolkena.

To Kay Stepp for her years of mentorship and wonderful encouragement.

To Simon Bailey for his constant inspiration and encouragement on this journey.

To Scott White for his unbelievable example of friendship, generosity, and constant ability to show up in life as his best self.

To Joe Zaniker for being an amazing friend and for loving me.

To Linda Devers for believing in me and going on several uncharted journeys with me and being so amazing through it all.

To Linda Mendenhall for a truly amazing relationship, two wonderful children, and her continued love and support.

To my son, Cooper, for being a loving, insightful, intuitive, lovely human being. To my son, Tucker, for being my constant playmate and lover of life. Thank you for making me laugh and showing me how to live each and every moment.

To my wonderful, loving partner Tim Healea for his beautiful example of how to live life full of Spark!

To my Mom and Dad for their love and support to go for it in life. To my sister and brothers, Linda, David, and Jeff, for their commitment to being a great family.

To my publisher, Suzanne Deakins, thank you for believing in me and making the process so great, no matter what obstacles we faced!

To my designer, Chad Harder, thank you for being such a great cheerleader and creating such a beautiful cover.

To Masha Alexander for showing up at the perfect time and proofreading on a moments notice.

To Linda Meyer for her outstanding copyediting and working into the wee hours with me.

To Bob Smith for his outstanding work handling the printing.

To Erick Petersen for being full of Spark and for being so coachable. Thank you for your friendship.

To Jeff Strode for being an amazing boss while I juggle a ton of different passions in life.

To Ron Destefano for your assistance and gentle guidance along the way.

To Brett Soulek for your insight, encouragement, and support.

To Trei Herd for calling me to action and being the magnificent person you are.

Foreword

You hold in your hands one of the most inspiring, engaging, and thought-provoking books ever written. Bookstore shelves are crammed with self-help books. However, **Spark!** does more than take up space. Doug has crafted a masterpiece that teaches you how to start a blazing fire with the match called **You**!

If your fire for living a meaningful life has gone out, read and internalize the stories and timeless truths in this incredible book. I am convinced that if you will allow the counsel contained herein to penetrate your soul, your life will never be the same again. You will find yourself nodding your head with a resounding "yes" to the life you were meant to live.

Take a quantum leap into a new reality and the unlimited future that awaits you. Feel the spark plugs of possibility ignite and drive you from the inside out.

Everyone you know needs a spark...let it begin with you!

Simon T. Bailey
Catalyst of Brilliance
Imagination Institute, Inc.

Introduction

What is spark?

Webster's dictionary defines spark as "a quality or feeling with latent potential and a vital, animating, or activating factor." That definition fits, but for the purposes of this book, I define spark as the gleam we exude when we are utterly fascinated by life, love, and people. Sparky people stand out in the world due to their infectious enthusiasm, effortless smiles, and unlimited energy.

They are easy to spot walking the streets of the world because their faces and energy are alive. Like everyone else, their daily worlds are filled with issues, challenges, and problems, but they have a way of living life that keeps them vibrant.

I noticed that people with spark didn't have to work hard to live like this—it is their natural way of living. For them to show up differently stands out as unusual rather than the other way around.

The beginnings

I started this project with the belief that nature, God, and the Universe want us to be amazing. It is our natural state to be full of spark! As young children, it was unnatural for us to be unhappy, miserable, and lonely. Those feelings showed up at times, but it was unnatural for us to stay down.

My passion for this project came from walking the streets of different cities in the world and taking time to observe people. I would play games as I walked. On one street, I would make eye contact with everyone I passed. Then, on the next street, I would say, "Hi, good morning." On the next street, I would just smile. The results of these games surprised me.

I noticed that most of us do not return eye contact, we reject greetings, and we frown at smiles. It seemed the larger the city, the worse the result.

How would the world be different if all of us walking down the street had a spark in our eye? What if all of us were passionate about our lives, our work, and the people in our lives? What would happen if we were more focused on how we were living rather than what we were doing? Could we change our world?

I grew up in a sparky household. My natural state of being was to connect with people. When I was a little boy, I would start knocking on the neighbors' doors as the moving van unloaded to see who wanted to come out and play.

It is my firm belief we are all born sparky and somehow, through living each day, most of us allow our enthusiasm to slowly drain. I interviewed an eighth-grader who brilliantly deduced, "We lose our spark because we start to worry about what other people think."

In this book, those who have allowed their spark to drift will find the path back to a natural state of passion, high energy, and joy. Those who are already full of passion will find a process to help increase their level of spark!

Interviewing one hundred and twenty of the most sparky people around the world benefited *my* level of spark. Each day I was inspired to be more capable, observant, and filled with life than I was the day before.

Everyone I interviewed was referred to me. My criteria? I wanted to speak to the one person everyone knew who was living life powerfully, with tremendous passion, energy and resilience. I was touched by how people thought differently than I did. I was inspired by their world views. I noticed how many of us are walking a purposeful path in life.

In this book, I have presented my observations about what creates spark. I have shared stories to show how this applies in everyday life. I have worked with great people to provide exercises to bring these elements into full effect within your life.

To test the process, I worked with many people over a seven-month period to help them regain their spark. During the process, I was so overwhelmed by what they were able to create in their lives that I became convinced anyone could recapture or enhance their spark. As a side benefit, all of these people found new meaning in their jobs. Each went from thinking his or her job was a big reason for their loss of spark, to seeing a new possibility that their job is a great avenue to express their spark!

Please join me in this mission to change the streets of the world. Let's increase the passion, joy, laughter, and love in this world we share. Make a daily commitment to practice the ten elements described in this book, and you will find your spark!

Doug Mendenhall,
Portland, Oregon, 2006

You can fulfill your purpose in everything you do in life, from how you show up at breakfast in the morning to how you do your job.

Chapter 1 - Purpose

When you are doing what you love to do, you never work a day in your life. —Simon Bailey

Definition:
Purpose involves so much. It captures who you want to be, what you want to be about, and where you want to apply your special abilities in the world. It is the unique reason you were put on this planet.

Getting clear about your purpose can energize your life. It provides the excitement to get out of bed every day and the commitment to see something through massive obstacles and challenges. Purpose is so much broader than what you do for a living.

You can fulfill your purpose in everything you do in life, from how you show up at breakfast in the morning to how you do your job. Once you become clear, you can approach each day with an intention of how you will impact that day. You will make decisions based on how they fit within your purpose.

Many books have been written about purpose, and I have read many of them. What absolutely stood out in my research was how committed the sparkiest people were to who they wanted to be in the world! They were not casual about it; they always sought to show up in arguments, in their jobs, and in their families as their best self, their Purposeful Self.

There has been a lot of discussion about purpose. Most of it centers on your calling and how to identify jobs that align with that calling.

What I find to be most important (to live passionately and enthusiastically) is to first define who you are committed to being in the world!

So, let's identify the three exciting components of purpose:

Purposeful Self. Who do you want to be? How do you want to show up during each moment in life? How do you want others to experience you? Who would you be as your best rendition of yourself?

Purposeful Calling. What is your mission? How do you want to change the world or interact with your neighborhood, your city, and your country? When you are being who you want to be, what are you committed to in life? What will you cause in the world?

Purposeful Endeavor(s). What is going to be your work? What groups are you going to join? What will be your day job(s)?

Many of us are concerned with our job. Before you spend any time deciding your job, first consider how to get clear on your Purposeful Self and your Purposeful Calling. After getting clear in these two areas, deciding your Purposeful Endeavor(s) is easy. You will find you have many options, including staying with your current job, to fulfill your purpose.

At the end of this chapter and in the workbook, we will go through some exercises that will help you uncover the three areas of purpose. Let's discuss the three areas of purpose further, so you can begin to think about how these apply in your life.

Purposeful Self. This is who you want to be, the kind of person others can expect to see when you arrive. It is who you are committed to being when you are at your best! You may fall into old patterns, but by having a written statement of who you are committed to being, you will have an opportunity to notice when you are showing up as less than your best self. As moments in your life are happening, you can bring this statement to mind and ensure you show up with all your brilliance.

An example of a Purposeful Self statement is: "When I am my best self, I show up as a warm, loving man full of enthusiasm, respect for others' choices, and a bias for action."

If I find myself in an argument and I am not being my best self—which is often how I find myself in the area of arguments—I can now ask myself the following question, right in the middle of the argument: "Am I more committed to winning this argument or more committed to being warm, loving, enthusiastic, respectful, and action-oriented?"

Purposeful Calling. This is what you care about creating in the world—it is your mission. If it truly reflects your calling, it will influence everything you do in your life. You will approach raising children, being a partner, working, coaching soccer, attending your local Elks chapter, and being a son or daughter differently. In every situation, you can see how it represents an opportunity to fulfill your unique purpose.

If you approach each situation as your best self, while understanding how it is in some way fulfilling your mission in life, it will give you such a sense of accomplishment that you are likely to start floating higher off the ground as you live your life.

What would life be like if you had this sense in everything you did? Who would you be if you were being that person? When you are clear about your purpose, your life flows and requires fewer struggles. When you are your best self, there is much less cleanup required in life, meaning you don't have to keep cleaning up the messy situations you create. Everything you do is heightened and it is easy to be passionate and enthusiastic about seemingly simple things.

An example of a Purposeful Calling statement is: "I am here to inspire people to see their brilliance and act on it."

Your calling can be incredibly simple. It may be easier to distill it to the one thing that really excites you in life. It is important to keep it broad enough that you can fulfill your calling in everything you do.

When I enter a situation conscious of my Purposeful Calling, I now know what to do; I used to be uncertain and confused. As an example, when asked to work on a board, I used to wonder what role I should take, or how I could add value. Now, I am completely clear that my role is to assist others in seeing their brilliance and take action. Being clear has simplified my life.

Purposeful Endeavor(s). This is what you actually get involved in that allows you the opportunity to live as your Purposeful Self and to live out your Purposeful Calling. This can be your job, hobbies, committees, clubs, being part of a family, walking down the street, and so forth. You can proactively seek endeavors that best fit your purpose. By having a clear, written purpose, you will notice groups and associations with which it makes sense to get involved. Your Purposeful Calling will influence everything, and endeavors will eventually appear that are closely aligned with your purpose.

Examples of Purposeful Endeavor(s) that can serve your Purposeful Self and Purposeful Calling are:

- Setting up a local Rotary chapter
- Writing books
- Serving as a business leader dedicated to employees' growth
- Running for political office to change the focus of state leadership
- Volunteering at the local HIV/AIDS hospice
- Coaching Little League
- Singing in choir

You may notice that you can choose any endeavor and have it relate to your Purposeful Self and Purposeful Calling, since it is more about how you approach the endeavor than about the endeavor itself. That is what is so powerful about being clear with your purpose. Potentially, you won't have to make any changes to your life, and yet you can have a completely different life.

How purpose affects spark:
When you live with purpose, it allows magic to enter seemingly simple times in your life. You can see how you saved someone's marriage because of how you showed up in a conversation. You notice how you altered the course of someone's life by asking two questions at the end of softball practice. It is important to think about this for a moment.

When you are clear about your calling and committed to being your best self, you will listen differently. You will notice opportunities to make a difference in the world. You will see how your actions impact everyone around you.

We all experience meaning in our lives from many sources, and some things, like being a parent, may provide lasting meaning. However, having a clear purpose can bring meaning to every moment of your life. For example, it can turn an otherwise uneventful cocktail party into an incredibly rewarding series of conversations. It can take an already meaningful area, such as parenting, and cause your effectiveness to skyrocket when you show up as your best self with an intention to live your calling.

Purpose is a powerful motivator to do great things. It provides definition to your life, so when you get lost or feel in a rut, you can rediscover meaning by renewing your purpose. When faced with a big decision, you can look at it with your purpose in full view. You can ask, "Can I fulfill my purpose best by doing this or not doing this? Does this job or that job best present an opportunity for me to live my calling? Given this group or that group to join, which best supports me in my purpose? How can I design my relationships to support me being my best self?"

Your purpose may grow and evolve over time. You may determine where it falls short of what you want to create, and slightly alter it. My original Purposeful Calling was to help others find their brilliance. I noticed that it was unsatisfying to have people comprehend their brilliance and do nothing with it, so I altered my calling as follows: "My calling is to assist others in seeing their brilliance and acting on it." By adding the piece about taking action, I bring a different intention, and it slants everything I do toward some action-oriented component.

It is important to notice that by having my Purposeful Calling clear, I was able to see that it needed to evolve to include action. It is important to write it down and get clear about each area of your purpose. Know who you want to be, how you want to show up, and what you want to do in life. Writing it down helps you focus; it brings clarity, which allows you to be conscious and make clear choices.

I always felt when someone said, 'you should do...' that it was someone else's game plan. I make sure it is my purpose. —Terri Watson.

You will likely be given advice from many people in your life, solicited and unsolicited. When you have your purpose clearly defined, it is much simpler to know which advice fits your life and which advice can be gratefully ignored. However, when you are without a clear understanding of your purpose, you are more likely to fall prey to someone else's game plan, and listen to what they think you should do.

Clarity about your purpose in life is such a gift to give yourself. You will immediately have more energy for what you do and understand why you are doing what you do. Many people go through their entire lives not knowing what they want to do. Unfortunately, they miss the passion that purpose can bring to life.

In the following section, I will present passionate people and share their stories. I will highlight how purpose works in their lives, how they each live their purpose, how they ensure purpose stays in their lives, and how it feels to have a clear purpose.

How purpose works in day-to-day living:

Cathy Hawk, founder of Clarity International

Cathy grew up in New Jersey, where her parents nicknamed her 'Reddi' after Reddi Kilowatt—the local electric company. They said it was because she always looked on the bright side of life. Cathy was fascinated with people and always asked questions. So much so that her father jokingly said he would not have another child.

Cathy was intentional from an early age. She liked helping those in need. In high school, she worked for Animal Rescue, a group dedicated to saving animals. In college, Cathy continued as a social activist, helping to sneak food to African-American students who were not allowed in restaurants. She helped them ride on the bus even though it was illegal. Cathy marched in Washington, D.C., in one of the first feminist rallies and was arrested with 8,000 other women.

Cathy's purposeful pursuit of making a difference in others' lives brought great passion to her life. That passion helped Cathy keep working even when big obstacles appeared. She simply could not be stopped. One example is her effort to help start the first-ever peer review board in the United States. It met with significant resistance and took heavy politicking, lobbying, and grass roots activism to bring change, but everyone stayed the course.

Cathy worked as a dental hygienist for twenty-eight years and found that she looked at the people connected to the teeth more than the teeth themselves. Cathy was an early pioneer in reading people's energy. She was curious why people did things, so she took classes on motivation and applied kinesiology.

When you are in your area of purpose, your curiosity is continually provoked because everything matters to you. Roadblocks must be passed, so you find ways around them.

Nearing a normal retirement age, Cathy received a lot of well-intentioned advice. Many friends told her what she should do, considering her age. They pointed out how soon she would be vested in her stock options.

Somewhere in the middle of her life, Cathy had accepted a societal story that she would do one thing, and then retire. The story she had bought into also said quitting meant you were a flake and not loyal. This acceptance had cost Cathy her curiosity after twenty years. Her mind wasn't as sharp. She was no longer innovative. She had become run of the mill.

Now, Cathy notices when her curiosity lags. She sees it as a clue to further refine her purpose and passionately re-engage. Cathy recognized that the advice given to her came from a place of fear. She knew what she was doing was too important to succumb to fear.

In the end, Cathy and her husband were most turned on by helping others determine exactly what was so difficult for them to figure out: where is my passion taking me now, what is my purpose, what is my vision? Through their own experiences, they had the beginnings of a methodology to read energy. They could perfect this process for others and significantly shorten the time required.

"We were having a ball! So we knew it was right. Our son commented on how we were different. He noticed his father always looked handsome in his suit before, but he also looked sad, and now he looked excited!"

Cathy and her husband have now been running Clarity International for nine years, and are fully engaged in their life's work. Cathy notices she and her husband look younger than years before, and they feel more alive and balanced. Cathy's purpose draws her forward, propelling her into her next challenge, her next discovery. And if ever her curiosity lags, she knows it is time to shake things up again.

How purpose may evolve over time:

John Chapman, Entrepreneur and Inspiration behind HeartSpark

John has long been interested in organizations and people, studying why they do what they do. One of his early efforts to help people be their fullest was to help his Navy Chief, who throughout his twenty-seven year Naval career, had had trouble writing performance reviews designed to help his people grow.

John was twenty-one years old and lacked knowledge in his career, but he had a passion for "growing people." He knew how his Chief should write those reviews, and took on the exciting task of helping people grow.

Eventually, it was time for John to leave the service. He left as a nuclear engineer and joined a local utility in the Northwest, but he was disappointed in American business. He felt it doused people's fire, losing much of why people came to America.

John noticed that companies ultimately perform by showing people how to get what they want, and then connecting that to helping the company get what it wants. John pursued roles where he could affect that vision, frequently moving around within a company.

He worked himself out of job after job, helping others move up. He loved it. John's purpose of helping others grow gave his life great meaning. It brought enthusiasm and joy to his work.

John went on to manage most of the key operations of the utility except for line crews. After some time, John became intrigued by a question: Were people doing what they were doing because of John's position or because they believed in John as well as what they were doing? John realized the only way he could truly answer that question was if he had zero positional power, so he decided to step out of the hierarchy. His boss was supportive, but as time passed, the organization's recognition kept shrinking, demonstrating dwindling appreciation for his less-visible contribution. Undeterred, John kept track of three measurable outcomes:

- Dependent Changes – things that changed because of conversations he had with people (e.g., Employee X was going to hit this person, but decided to write a letter instead).

- Independent Changes – where people learned through their interaction with John and made a decision in the future based on that learning.

- Interdependent Changes – where people took leadership responsibility in order to fuel an idea between groups, and it happened without John. These were the most valuable yet hardest to measure because the best ones owned the result so much they failed to inform John (he had to discover them on his own by walking around).

John was pleased with the progress and the results. Unfortunately, the company didn't see the same value and decided to lay John off. John saw this as a blessing, as it allowed him to focus entirely on what he really loved to do, help other people grow.

Since John's purpose was clear, getting laid off didn't deter him. He not only found another way to stay with his purpose, he found living his purpose even more fulfilling. John is now getting to a place where he sees compensation as more than money. He sees feedback as a greater reward than dollars.

"It is about deprogramming myself from the part of our culture that says money measures my worth. I figure my job is not about fixing, but enabling what is already there. I help people listen to themselves."

John's purpose led him to co-found HeartSpark, which helps people become more purposeful by knowing who they are (their natural success patterns), by knowing what they want (most people are very unclear about this), and by knowing why they are here. John feels purpose isn't "out there," it is in the moment; you are choosing it daily.

John used to state his purpose as helping others see things in the way of their desired growth and doing something about it. Initially, he found it satisfying listening to others and asking questions to help them discover opportunities hidden in their problems.

However, it soon became less satisfying because John was always drawing in problems. John learned he did not have to begin with problems to find positive opportunities. He changed his purpose to be an insightful mirror for positive self-discovery. This was significant as now John could help people without the distraction of problems.

It is important to get started by writing down your first concept of Purposeful Self and Purposeful Calling (exercises at the end of the chapter will help you draw this out).

As you think about purpose, begin by noticing good feelings inside when you are being meaningful for others. When you are clear that things are working well for you, you feel valuable and you know you are making a meaningful difference. In those moments, you have the unique opportunity to notice what your purpose is. You are purposeful in those moments!

Our individual collection of meaningful moments is our reason for being. When we feel this good we ask ourselves: What am I creating for others right now? How might the world be different if everyone had access to that part of me all the time? When you start listening, you can fine-tune your written version and continue to refocus your life for more meaning.

John thinks that if we could catch ourselves in the eight-to-ten-year-old range, before we start basing our values on what other people think, then we might mature faster and gain earlier insight into our purpose. John understands that much of the skill in finding purpose begins with the questions we are willing to ask ourselves and asking them at the right time.

To help people discover their purpose, some of the questions John likes to ask are: What do people tend to come to me for wherein I know I am most helpful? (There is a pattern to those paths to our door.) When I find myself feeling good because someone just thanked me for being so helpful, what was the effect I created? What type of help did I just provide?

"Being intentional draws opportunities to you. If you become clear about what you want, things show up. Purpose is active. I am on purpose. It's a feeling. I think we can feel it when we are on purpose. You know it because you feel good, you know you matter, that you make a difference."

How purpose calls forth new possibilities:

Dr. José Zaglul, President of Earth University in Costa Rica

José grew up in a very spiritual family. His parents were committed to giving their children a better life and education, so the whole family moved from Lebanon to Costa Rica when José was six years old. "I felt so fortunate that my father gave up his country for us. If I had grown up in Lebanon, we would have been struggling farmers, and I would not have the opportunities that I do now."

José went to college in Beirut. He knew the world needed to learn to live together. While in college, war broke out, and José saw how under unjust conditions people who were otherwise peaceful could be caught up in an environment and cycle of violence. He committed himself to bringing harmony and cooperation to the world.

"If we get the right leadership, with the right attitude, we might have a chance. My concern is that without visionary leadership, it will take a severe crisis, like disease or war, to bring about the changes we need in the world. I don't believe that we should have to go through a tragedy to learn. If we can think longer term, we could be a better society. I want to see us share with one another, live peacefully, and be less materialistic."

While working at the Costa Rican Technology Institute, one of four state universities in Costa Rica, José considered quitting academia altogether due to the number of barriers. He was frustrated because it was so difficult to make changes. When EARTH University was first proposed with funding from international organizations, José opposed the idea because he saw it as a foreign institution motivated by a political agenda. Later on, when he learned more about the mission and saw its potential to generate change in Latin America through education, he decided to apply for the position of the President. He was one of eighty candidates from around the world considered for the position.

"I was sure I would not be hired, so I did not hide anything; I was just myself. I said everything that came to mind, including my doubts about the institution, and it worked."

Following your purpose presents challenges and roadblocks.

You will be faced with big decisions, just as Dr. Zaglul was. However, if what you are doing is tied into your purpose, each choice (which seems so critical because it matters to you) will reveal your next choice. It is so important to keep choosing and to stay in action.

José's purpose was to inspire people to be agents of change leading to a world of harmony. At EARTH University, the board allowed him freedom that was different from other universities. José found his purpose nurtured by new hopes. He saw how he and his students were changing the world. He saw opportunities to teach other universities and create a multiplying effect.

"The energy was wonderful. We were able to channel it to not only say something to the world, but to also behave accordingly, allowing others to witness us."

When you continue in your purpose, and you continue to make choices, opportunities to be more effective leap out at you.

One particular student shines for José as a prime example of how EARTH University is helping change the world. This student was an extremely poor indigenous youth from Tuxtepec-Oaxaca, Mexico. Prior to his entrance interview in the capital, he had never set foot in a hotel. His academics had substantial deficiencies, but he had an amazing energy and commitment to help his community. A philanthropist from Mexico provided a scholarship for him.

The student was told to focus on academics due to his deficiencies, but he was deeply dedicated to the community and to working with the poor. One of his projects involved organizing other students to make thirty toy cars for poor children during Christmas. His first year was a struggle and he barely made it. His second year he continued to struggle, and his third year he flunked out of school and had to leave.

The philanthropist who had sponsored him was convinced that it was worthwhile to give this kid a second chance. The University arranged for the student to live with a family in the nearby community, which he had helped while he was enrolled at EARTH University. During his year off, he lived and worked in the community, while professors on campus provided him with materials and classes to improve academically. He was admitted the following year and two years later he graduated.

José did not hear from him for five years, but then received a gift from him, followed by a phone call. It turns out he was the Assistant Director General of the Municipality in Tuxtepec-Oaxaca where he was in charge of a sustainable development program. He had implemented a recycling system and opened numerous city parks. As a result of his contributions, he was given a key to the city.

"If we had not given him a chance, he would be picking strawberries, but now he is a star. He is changing his country and his people. He is sending more students as well. It is a beautiful example how changes can happen for kids like this."

All of this happened because José continued to uncover his purpose. He made choices, faced roadblocks, and made new choices. His result is a passionate, fulfilling life where he feels the difference he is making in the world.

"All of us have to do our best for the future of this planet. We cannot be silent! Even if it is beyond my influence, I speak out and allow others to convince me or be convinced by me."

How purpose has a momentum that builds confidence:

Chuck Collins, Doer in Life, Founder of United for a Fair Economy, Father, Spouse, and Active Member in the Local Community

Chuck grew up in a 'can-do' family. His father encouraged him to do something about problems he uncovered. In science class, Chuck's teacher discussed pollution and its effect on the world. Chuck shared his passion about pollution with his father, who suggested they make a leaflet. His father's encouragement helped Chuck see his role in making a difference.

They made one hundred copies and took them around in Chuck's wagon to all the neighbors. People remembered it for years. It gave Chuck confidence as a child. Ten years later, Chuck was part of a movement that successfully shut down the Seabrook Nuclear Power Plant in New Hampshire.

When you see yourself making a difference in something that matters to you, it naturally brings enthusiasm to your life that builds on itself.

"I see that when there is a lot of toil involved in getting something done, it squeezes the hope out of people. They stop believing that they can make a difference."

Chuck personally has several purposes going in his life, and feels fortunate when they happen to line up together. One of his current purposes is to deal with advertising in our culture and its impact on girls. This lines up with his role as a father. One of his missions is to encourage fathers to prepare their daughters about body image by discussing what is important about their bodies.

What is so important about Chuck is that he takes action. His action brings changes and reinforces that what he is doing really matters. When you see how you are making a difference for other people, it keeps you going and brings great excitement to your life.

In the last five years, Chuck has paid attention to his frustrations and impatience, noticing that these are clues—signs that he is off course. For example, he had been serving on a board, and it had become an obligation rather than a desire to go to the meetings. Chuck found himself becoming impatient, which he took as a clue that he no longer belonged there. He sensed that it was not part of his calling, so his energy and passion were not present.

He chose to make a graceful exit and continue listening to where he should focus his energy. He notices this brings new teachers into his life.

"In the past, I would seek out what I was supposed to do, the notion of my calling. Now, I realize it isn't mine to figure out, so I just listen."

As you look at each of these passionate people, you can see each one finds his or her purpose and calling in different ways. However, what they all have in common is a continued listening or noticing of how they are fulfilling a purpose. This keeps them going and keeps them engaged in their lives in powerful and enthusiastic ways.

It is also important to share how much fun these people have along the way. They live with great joy during the process of making a difference.

Chuck sees that all his prior journeys prepared him for his work now. He didn't see it as it happened along the way, but now he knows there were no unnecessary side trips. Chuck believes all people can change; no one is permanently stuck.

15

"The past is determined, but the future is our free will. History shows us that individual actions add up to big changes. I allow myself to think BIG and I always want to be a participant."

How purpose brings meaning and excitement to life:

Fran Korten, Networker for Social Change, Executive Director of Positive Futures Network and *YES! Magazine*

Fran has spent most of her life out of the United States, working in Ethiopia, Nicaragua, and Southeast Asia. In high school, the book *The Ugly American* heavily influenced her. The book discussed how, due to their arrogance, Americans abroad did not take the time to understand the local people. Fran wanted to be different. At this time, the Peace Corps did not exist, so Fran had to find a way to get involved.

Notice that Fran's purpose called her into action. Affecting the world outside America mattered to Fran.

Fran set off to Nicaragua in 1970 to set up health programs. Birth control was a new idea and most people had not heard about it. Fran found out most of the local women wanted fewer children than they had, which was counter to what many experts expected. Fran also saw the family planning provided by the government was inadequate.

Fran's choices allowed her to see new ways to make a difference.

There were long waits, and clinics were far away from the villages. There was a disconnect between the government offering and the demand for the services. The government treated the women as if they were doing them a big favor rather than serving their needs.

"I came to these countries with a naïve notion. I thought I would come in and help them. What I learned was that these villages had great capacity to solve their own problems, but they were being ignored."

Fran was encouraged in her ability to make a difference, so she continued. She saw the possibility of a more effective partnership between the local people and the helping organization.

For example, in the Philippines, farmers had been irrigating for centuries. The government arrived and said they would help by building better dams. They sent in surveyors who proceeded without talking to the farmers. Everything was from the top down. The government was trying to help the group, but, in many cases, ended up undermining the existing social structures.

When dams were moved, it changed the structure of the irrigation association that needed to maintain the system. Fran and others worked to change this by supporting the government in organizing the community prior to the surveyors and engineers appearance. They then worked together to solve the problems.

Fran highlights the importance of seeing others as equals. If a government official sees a barefoot farmer as inferior, then no opportunity for learning exists. Equality, which allows learning from everyone, opens up new opportunities to be effective in your purpose.

Fran's purpose is to create dignity for everyone, where everyone understands his or her value and has a say.

Fran's passion about changing the world led her to a new opportunity at the Positive Futures Network. They publish *YES! Magazine*, which is all about solutions and action. Since Fran is living her purpose, exciting new doors keep opening for her. Of course, Fran is able to see them and dives right in.

"It keeps me young. I am sixty-two years old, and I have more energy than ever. I am driven by my passions, so I learn what I need to. I get to hang around the best people and call them my friends. It really is incredible. It keeps life fun, and as my good friend Grace Boggs says, the future is so exciting because we don't know what is going to happen."

How you can uncover your purpose:
This is a big question, and one that many people struggle with their whole lives. It is important to understand the difference between how you want to live your life versus what your job is. Many people I interviewed found that by changing the way they lived their lives, they could live their purpose doing the same thing they were doing before. By focusing on how they showed up in life and what their driving missions were, their unfulfilling jobs suddenly came to life.

So, how do you find your passion and decide what you want to do with your life? Let's explore how to flush out your Purposeful Self, Calling, and Endeavors. There are several theories on how best to find your purpose.

The following method works extremely well. You will uncover the most important things to you and what holds you back, and this will help you form your three areas of purpose. If you have the workbook, pull it out now and complete the following exercise. Otherwise, complete these exercises in a notebook that you keep for all your spark work.

1) Clearly state how you want to show up in life for others. This will help you identify your Purposeful Self. You will uncover who you want to be and how you want others to feel when they are around you. Take out a pad and pencil, and answer the following questions,

- At **my funeral**, how do I wish people felt when they were around me? Don't try to guess how they feel now. This is about what you ideally want them to feel. It doesn't have to be based on reality.

- After a long weekend with the **most special person** in my life, how would I want them to describe how they felt being with me? Think of the most wonderful things they could say about how they felt and write those down.

- The **children in your life** (even if they are not your own) after spending the most ideal day with you, would say

18

what about how they felt? Imagine you had the most special time playing with children and they just enjoyed it more than anything, how would they feel?

Stop here and notice if your answers are the same for all three questions. Comment on why they are the same or different. Spend some time thinking about your answers.

2) Things you notice about yourself. Answer the following:

- My best qualities are...

- I shine when....

- I am most myself when...

Stop here and let's create your Purposeful Self statement. Look at your answers to the questions in exercise 1 and see the words people used to describe how they felt when they were with you. Add to that the answers you gave for exercise 2.

Group these words into main categories. For example, if you notice the words enthusiastic, happy, and energized, put them all in one category. If you notice the words loving, concerned, compassionate, put them in another category. Try to put all the words/descriptors into four or five main word categories. Group words that are connected in some manner.

Now, select and circle the word that means the most to you within each category. Use these words to create a Purposeful Self statement.

For example, if graceful, love, and inspire were your three most meaningful words, then your Purposeful Self statement might read, "I am a graceful, loving woman here to inspire other human beings."

This statement can now be used to encourage you to show up in that capacity more often. It can also be used to guide you back to the person you want to be if you should lose sight of your purpose.

3) Be clear about what you want to do in your lifetime. This seems simple enough, but most people don't take the time to do this critical step. This will help you identify your Purposeful Calling. Take out a pad and pencil, and answer the following questions:

- I **excel** at...

- The **activities I love** now are...

- What I **do effortlessly** is...

- I am **repeatedly drawn** to...

- If you were to be of **service in life**, what would you naturally be good at?

- If I knew this was my **last twenty-four hours on earth**, what would I want to do? Describe in some detail what you would want to do**.** After you write down your answers, test them. Ask yourself: If you were saying goodbye right now, would you feel complete? If not, go back and redo the list until you *would* feel complete.

- If I knew this was my **last five years on earth**, what would I want to do?

- Assuming an average life expectancy of seventy-seven years of age, how much lifetime do you have left? **What would you do with your life if that were your time remaining?** Take your time to think through this question and make sure that is what you would really do.

Stop here and notice what changes in your answers as the timeline extends from twenty-four hours to several years. At what time horizon do you start to lose the urgency? Are there any items on your list that are what other people think you should do, but don't speak to you?

Recheck the list and make it exclusively about what really matters to *you*. Group your answers at a higher level.

For example, if you would spend time with your kids teaching them everything you know, if you would spend time teaching a course on history, and if you would spend time volunteering to teach mentally challenged people how to run track and field, then list all of those under teaching, etc. Repeat this until you have effectively grouped your answers into four or five categories. Circle the most important categories.

4) Remove all possible barriers and notice which barriers affect you. This exercise will identify what holds you back. If you don't think you'd do anything different, mark "Not Applicable" to that question. Take out a pad and pencil, and answer the following questions:

- What would you do if only you were healthier?
- What would you do if only you were younger?
- What would you do if only you had more energy?
- What would you do if only you had more time?
- What would you do if only you had more money?
- What would you do if you knew you would not be rejected?
- What would you do if no one else had to know?
- What would you do if you knew you could not fail?

Stop here and identify which of these questions literally would cause you to do something different. If this reason holds you back from doing what you really want to do, spend some time figuring out why this reason is so significant to you. Write down your answer.

Now, let's create your Purposeful Calling. First, let's start with your categories from exercise 3. Add items from exercise 4. Create a new category if something important does not fit into an existing one.

For example, if you see traveling, seeing different people, cultures, exploring, and discovering, put all of those into one category and label it with the word that speaks to you most strongly. If you see training, coaching, and working with people, then put all of those into another category and label it with the word that speaks to you the most strongly.

After you have finished grouping everything you have a desire to do in life, go back through the categories and be selective. Narrow the number of categories down to the ones that really matter to you and cross out the other categories. If you cannot cross out any categories, then this is okay too.

Now, select the word/descriptor that means the most to you within each category. Use these to create a Purposeful Calling statement.

For example, if your most important categories were leadership, empowerment, and helping others discover their magic, then your Purposeful Calling statement might read: "I am here to be an energetic leader who empowers people to see and act on the magic within themselves."

This statement can now be used to influence how you approach each role or job in life. It can also be used to guide you on choices you face each day, evaluating how each choice fits your calling.

5) Brainstorm your Purposeful Endeavors. Now that you have created your Purposeful Self and Purposeful Calling, identifying Purposeful Endeavors should be much simpler.

Create a list of all the endeavors or lines of work you could pursue that would fit your Purposeful Calling. Review your answers in the first four exercises to see if any endeavors were listed. Spend some time really thinking of areas you could go into. Enlist friends and family to help you.

How does your current line of work fit your calling? Could it be a good fit if you approached it differently?

Notice if the items on your list are full-time focuses or if some are part-time efforts. Identify and circle the items on your list that are the best fit to your Purposeful Calling. You should notice that there is a wide variety of options for serving your calling. You will notice that you could show up to any of these endeavors as your Purposeful Self. Now you can choose which endeavors to pursue and begin to focus on your purpose in full consciousness!

Refine your Purposeful Self and Purposeful Calling statements by saying them out loud to different groups of people. Keep modifying these statements until they really speak to you. This exercise will help you clarify your purpose, develop enthusiasm, and signal your first actions. Over time, it will serve as a test to clarify whether your purpose continues to fulfill you. This may provide clues on when subtle or not-so-subtle changes are needed.

Powerful grounding questions:
Are you more committed to being your best self or being right? What experience do you leave people with after spending time with you? What do you cause in the world? What problems are worth committing your life to solving? Who are you committed to being?

Signs of excellence:
The biggest sign you are living on purpose is when everything flows. You will notice what you are doing makes sense.

How you are living will fit beautifully into everything around you. You can use this sense of flow as an indicator. If something shakes this balanced flow significantly, it is likely a sign that an evolution is happening or needs to happen for you to grow and continue learning.

Begin to notice the people you draw into your life. When your purpose is clear, you will draw in great teachers, interested students, and like-minded colleagues to assist you in your journey. This will make your life more fun. Your experience will be richer and your shared vision will expand.

Your teachers, students, and colleagues will help you see things about yourself that you might miss or might not recognize as special gifts. Don't miss the lessons that they highlight for you.

Create your life so you recognize the magic and joy in everyday happenings.

Chapter 2 - Attitude

Life is worth living, and today is my best day. —Lori Wisbeck

Definition:
Attitude is your chosen way of seeing life as you greet each moment. The choices you make affect how the world looks. It can be dark and dreary, complicated and scary, or the same world can be bright and full of possibility, simplicity, and wonder. Attitude is a filter through which you view the world, and choosing your attitude so that life works for you is powerful.

Most people are not aware of the attitudes they carry and how these attitudes affect their perceptions. In this chapter, we will focus on exposing your attitudes and discuss recommended attitudes that allow your enthusiasm and passion for life to thrive! You will see you have complete control over the attitudes through which you filter the world. You will see how the same world can look completely different depending on which attitude you select.

As you read this chapter, consider several questions: Are you completely clear how your attitudes create the world you see? Is it possible for two people to see the same world in completely different ways, one full of possibility and the other with little opportunity?

How do you approach unknown situations? How do you approach strangers? How do you respond when you become afraid? How do you handle criticism? How do you create disappointments in your life?

You may not be completely aware, but if you think about your answers to these questions, your attitudes will begin to reveal themselves. Once we reveal our attitudes, we can evaluate how well they serve us. We will uncover your attitudes in more depth during the exercises at the end of this chapter. So, put aside the questions for now, as we will come back to them.

How attitude affects spark:

If there was one thing that all of those interviewed had in common, it was a positive outlook. Your choice of attitude will affect your ability to see life as magic and abundant. Everyone I interviewed felt life was going to be great. They all had their favorite ways of adjusting and learning to focus their attitudes as they met each moment, but they all *lived in "the glass is full."*

This is especially important during trying situations. Real spark survives disappointment, and these people viewed disappointments as occasions for learning versus justification for withdrawal. Think about that for a moment. Why is that important?

Do you ever view disappointments as a justification to withdraw, quit, or retreat? What if you viewed them as lessons that made you that much more likely to succeed in your next attempt? How might that serve you? The attitudes you choose are vital to how you will proactively and reactively live your life.

Why is that the case? If you view a disappointment as an opportunity to learn, you will seek evidence that you are moving forward and growing in your dreams and purpose.

However, if you view a disappointment as a reason to withdraw, you will gather evidence as to how that area of your life is never going to work. The evidence will continue to mount until you convince yourself and everyone in your life that you cannot succeed.

It is easy to make the case that attitude is critical to achieve high levels of spark. It affects everything from the people you draw into your life, to your ability to achieve your purpose, to how you greet each moment as it arrives.

What a gift to become aware of the attitude you have chosen and to consider altering it if you can be better served with a new one.

How your world is created by the attitude you choose:

Susan Clark, Founder of HeartSpark

Ever since Susan was a little girl, she has had a strong belief that the universe is friendly. She has always felt special and chosen, but not in a way that singled her out from others. Susan has lived her life seeing everyone as special and unique in his or her own way.

This was the attitude from which Susan chose to live her life.

At age five, Susan remembers sleeping in the backyard with her sister. They saw a shooting star, and Susan knew she was supposed to make a wish. She didn't want to waste it, so it had to be a good one.

"I remember wishing everyone in the world could be 'as happy as I am right now.'"

This wish continues to be Susan's standard wish every time she blows out candles on her birthday cake or throws a penny in the wishing well. The responsibility of that wish is enormous. Susan recognizes that she has to be really happy or it isn't a great wish!

You can see how Susan is responsible for her happiness. She decides how to receive what life gives her and create happiness from whatever that is. Do most adults choose this attitude?

Susan kept that wish a secret until her parents' fiftieth wedding anniversary. "I told them because I wanted them to know my happiness was such an incredible gift. I was so fortunate to have their support. They always taught us that we could do anything if we put our mind to it."

While Susan had great support from her parents, many people I spoke with did not. However, they understood the power they created in their lives by choosing attitudes that caused their lives to be spectacular.

It isn't that Susan didn't have crises in her life. Susan has faced serious challenges. She listed fifteen major crises, and any one of them would knock the legs out from most people.

"I didn't want to live in the attitude of 'poor me' because it was depressing and it could affect my whole life. I didn't want to live in the negative. I wanted to be deliberate about getting beyond the crises."

What is so amazing about Susan is how consciously she chooses her attitude during the most difficult times in her life.

Her friends tried to be helpful, telling her: "You have to get through the dark times to appreciate the good times," "you are never given anything that you can't handle," and "you are being tested." Susan didn't believe any of these things. She believes some things just happen, the universe and God are friendly, there is no testing, and there is no dark side.

"I focused heavily on choosing my attitude. I wanted to keep my laugh through it all."

Susan never considered people evil, but she wanted to gain clarity on why some people choose the way they do. She studied the derivation of the words "sin" and "evil."

She found that sin is an archery term meaning "to miss the mark." The intention was good, but the mark was missed. She found that evil means "unripe." In terms of people, she felt this meant they hadn't blossomed into their good part yet.

Susan took each of her fifteen crises one by one, each separate from the other. She saw the crises were caused by a mark being missed or by ripening that was yet to occur.

You can see the power in how Susan chooses her attitude. She sees the same world through those eyes. She isn't blindly optimistic, but she sees the positive view of the world. Susan creates a life that she loves.

This requires Susan to have a practice of noticing her attitude. When she has a negative attitude, she works to replace it. For her, it is usually based on unfounded fears.

"Sometimes I will sing, loud and bad, but I sing. There is some kind of endorphin thing going on. I am a big believer in positive language, so I write and recite affirmations to myself. Other times, I will put on motivational tapes and books. I figure if I can't think positive on my own, I'll tap into someone who can."

Susan knows her attitude is not the normal attitude, but it makes her life easier. She expects magic to happen, and she expects the world is conspiring to give her everything she wants.

In addition to choosing her attitude during tough times, Susan creates spark in her everyday choices. For example, Susan makes a conscious effort to have her expression-at-rest be a smile. And, she challenges everyone to try it.

"It's not easy, but if you practice smiling when you are alone and when you go to the grocery store and when you walk down the street, it changes EVERYTHING, including how you feel inside and how the world responds to you."

Like everyone, Susan faces routine challenges in life. However, she stands out due to her conscious responses. How can you follow her example of finding an attitude that makes your life work? Specifically, how can you choose an attitude that allows for magic? How would your life change?

Susan's work, HeartSpark, introduces her view of the world to other people. The "Ten Personal Success Practices," developed with her partner, are her way of making good on the wish that everyone in the world be as happy as she is right now.

It is no coincidence that Susan was referred to me as someone that brings magic into the room.

How attitude can play a powerful role in how you interpret life:

Mickey Connolly, Founder and CEO, Conversant

Mickey grew up being very close to his mother. His father struggled as a big league baseball player after he had a serious auto accident right as he was called up to the majors. His parents divorced when he was three, and Mickey's mom moved them to Houston to start over.

Others may have viewed Mickey's situation as difficult, but he never had a memory of scarcity.

"We lived in Houston without a fan for five years, let alone air conditioning. We didn't know we were suffering, we just felt great."

How did Mickey's attitude affect how he interprets life? Could the rest of us interpret the same events differently?

Mickey's mom always believed things turned out for the best. "I always thought it was sappy. She was almost embarrassing, she was so positive," laughs Connolly. Even not having a father seemed fine to Mickey. He never knew he needed one.

Mickey's mom held down three jobs to get her kids through private school. They attended Our Lady of Mount Carmel High School. At school, the slogan on the seal stated, "It is not allowed to us to be mediocre."

Mickey loved that saying. It became one of two important attitudes in his approach to life. The second was his desire to find abundance regardless of his circumstances. "To me, abundance means whatever I need exists at the intersection of my talents and my situation."

Mickey's talent to choose his attitude during almost any situation allows him to interpret life in a way that really works. He gets to have abundance where others might see little opportunity. For example, to him, not having a father was great; he didn't know he needed one.

This concept is very simple. We all have complete control over what attitude we hold. The key is to notice. It provides power in creating your view of life, and your attitude affects everything. It affects the other people in your life and the opportunities you see in front of you.

Through Mickey's schooling and home life, he learned it was unacceptable to put up with things not working. Pain and suffering had to be overcome.

"It is more than being positive. It is being blessedly annoyed when things are not working."

Mickey always liked the TV show "MacGyver" because no matter what situation MacGyver was in, he could figure it out. MacGyver always focused on what life gave him versus what was wrong.

"That is a source of enormous excitement to me; it says that in any situation I can make it work. I don't have to be a victim."

How does the attitude of "any situation can work" create Mickey's life? How does having this attitude cause Mickey to interpret the world?

Mickey feels uncomfortable taking credit for his attitude. "My friend states that we don't raise ourselves, and I believe that. I was raised by a community that had confidence in living with faith in life."

This highlights the opportunity we all have to make a difference in our community. We can instill in each other the confidence to make any situation work. It is noticeable how Mickey is able to choose his attitude. That choice is available to him because he has practiced it his entire life.

Twenty years ago, Martin Buber, a Jewish theologian, touched Mickey. Buber wrote about the essential reciprocity of being. "To me that says we are not separate beings; we need each other. And, it is essential, not optional. I would not be aware of myself without you around me, so I better treat you like gold. We are reciprocal. I can change something in me that affects you."

Mickey points out that we matter to each other. We can see ourselves clearly by having other people around us. The attitude we choose affects everyone in our lives, and it affects their experiences of life.

Growing up in a musical family, Mickey sees life musically.

"I notice if I am in rhythm. I try to be conscious of flowing with life's rhythm."

As an example, one of Mickey's employees came to him stating, "Everyone says that we are in a bad economy. I believe the economy is different, not bad. It's like the band was playing the foxtrot and then switched to the mambo, but we are still doing the foxtrot. How do we dance with this economy?"

Mickey was reminded of MacGyver and how everything was there in that moment if he chose to notice what life was offering.

How does it work to hold an attitude of curiosity and an attitude of seeing the opportunity? How would life be different if the attitude of "why is this happening to me" was present?

Today, Mickey notices when some version of "we're in a bad economy" shows up in his life. Mickey wants to leverage his perception as an asset. He is studying how he can notice his initial reaction, and then alter the way he perceives life.

For example, when Mickey first started dating his wife, he was falling asleep during her opera performance. He didn't want to make a bad impression, so he fought to stay alert. She asked him what was going on after the performance and he said, "I was trying to enjoy the opera."

She corrected him, "No, you were trying to endure it. If you really were trying to enjoy the opera, you would look for the things that others enjoy. You'd look for what I enjoy. I think you only saw why you didn't like opera, and that will definitely put you to sleep."

Mickey asked himself, "Is my perception of the opera caused by the opera or me?" What Mickey concluded was that his perception of the opera was more available to him than he thought. The questions he asked determined his perceptions. If he asked, "What is wrong with opera?" he noticed how that governed the value he saw in it.

Mickey explored this concept further with a voicemail example. He asked several clients to select a recent voicemail they considered annoying. He had them listen to it four times, each time asking themselves one of the following four questions:

1. What is wrong with this person?

2. What is important for me to learn here?

3. Why do I have to deal with this?

4. What is this person trying to contribute?

His clients said it was like listening to four completely different voicemails. It was actually the same voicemail, but their perception changed based on the questions they asked themselves.

How can you notice when your life is not working, and instead of reacting, ask youreself a powerful question? How is attitude a factor? What other ways of viewing life are available right now?

Mickey continues to find the opportunity in what life gives him.

"Remember how Fred Astaire could dance with anything. One of his most famous dance scenes was with a chair. The story goes that he was returning to practice in the studio and someone had left a chair out. He didn't see the chair. When he came to that spot, he didn't get angry or annoyed, he simply incorporated the chair into his dance and kept going. It turned out to be the best part of the dance. I love that. It says to me, if I can just see what life is giving me and keep going, I can make that same magic. I may not be Fred Astaire, but I know that I can dance."

How attitude affects the joy available to you:

Laura Stepp, Mother and Strategic Programs & Organization Development Manager for Intel

Laura's parents said she was born with a special twinkle in her eye. Her report cards contained the terms energetic and bubbly.

She was brought up in a household that did not allow the word "can't," only "won't."

She was encouraged to show true grit and do whatever it took to make things happen. Her father taught her the value of discipline and staying focused, and her mother taught her to believe in her own unlimited potential.

In fifth grade, Laura had a fantastic teacher who was all about joy. He loved learning and loved kids. As a class, they put on radio shows and earned special points with creative projects. Her teacher believed everyone could do whatever he or she imagined. He believed everyone was equal and capable.

Laura's teacher stood out because of one attitude he held, that people's ability is unlimited. He gave them permission to try things and experiment. For Laura, it is a precious memory of a joyous time in life. How do your attitudes create room for joy in your life? In other's lives?

As Laura moved on to college, she had an opportunity to work over the summer helping an elderly blind lady write her life story.

"Mrs. Zelditch had spark. We ended up being great buddies. We would share dinner together and enjoy in-depth talks. I loved connecting with someone two generations away. At over ninety years of age, Mrs. Zelditch still had big dreams. Her attitude was to see the possibilities that life continued to offer. I was lucky to see such an amazing role model on how to grow old so beautifully."

Mrs. Zelditch stood out because she held an attitude that life is always full of possibilities. This gave her unlimited opportunities where joy was available, making her stand out from most people, even those half her age.

Moving out of college, Laura realized she buried things. It was part of her view of true grit and gutting things out. "I guess that was the down side to true grit. I'm still learning to release the less positive things and not hide them," laughs Laura.

People with spark have their own trials in life. What is different is how they move through these trials. There is a consistent attitude of "everything can work, anything can be figured out, and opportunity is everywhere." The wonderful realization is that this same attitude is available to everyone in the world.

Laura continued spending much of her young adult life trying to be perfect. "I now see you can't be perfect, but I had an expectation of what should be. That was my perfection. I couldn't reach it, and I didn't want to fail. After all, I really believed it wasn't okay not to do my very best. When my divorce happened, I lost myself for a couple years. I had always had a goal in my sights, and for the first time I had no goal. It's like I stopped seeing in color, and could only see black and white."

Laura knew she had to get out and reenergize herself and her attitude. She decided to dance. She immersed herself in country dancing, finding it a great release. Dancing required a total focus on the activity; she didn't have to think. It was exhilarating. She lost thirty-five pounds and burned the stress away. After two years, Laura realized to find balance in her life, she had to cut back on dancing and allow more room for other things. Dancing had served its purpose.

"When I am consumed by something like dancing, it is easy to have spark. It is easy to just get completely absorbed and passionate about the task. Now, I think the key is to have spark when your life is in balance. I try to sit longer and see what there is for me to learn. I am still working on this. Luckily, I am not dead yet," she laughs.

Laura has much more trust that her passion will come back when it goes missing. She has more trust that the right people will show up when needed. Laura's confidence comes from having practiced.

"The older I get, the more conscious I am about the rhythm of my attitude and what affects it. I am trying to be more authentic in more situations. Being around different people allows me to notice and pay attention to what I am bringing to the situation."

For her children, Laura wants to bring all she can to their lives. Laura used to feel that fear of failure was the best motivator. It motivated her to significant achievements in her life, but now she notices how joy and passion motivate her.

Laura notices that fear motivated her in the short term, but the motivations of joy and passion can sustain a person over a long period of time.

"When I am doing something I love, I don't even know I am doing anything. It is a completely different feeling, and it is so easy."

How you can create an attitude that works:

After enjoying the philosophies of each interviewee, the thought of combining them seems especially powerful in creating an amazing attitude for a great life. In this chapter, we will define attitudes that bring spark into your life and contrast them with attitudes that generally create the opposite.

As we discuss the attitude that generates spark, we will discuss how it is distinct from its opposing attitude. We will talk about what is available for you in life by choosing the attitude of spark.

The following are attitudes that create spark and their counterparts:

- *Gratitude* vs. *Entitlement*
- *Freedom* vs. *Attachment*
- *Journey-Orientation* vs. *Task-Orientation*
- *Fascination* vs. *Know-It-All*
- *At Choice* vs. *Victim*
- *Inclusion* vs. *Competition*
- *Excellence* vs. *Perfection*
- *Humor* vs. *Seriousness*
- *Passion* vs. *Withdrawal*
- *Confidence* vs. *Uncertainty*

Gratitude – choosing an attitude of gratitude allows for appreciating everything that comes your way, including difficulties. How can you see everything as a gift? How would your life be if you were grateful for each moment?

Being grateful allows for positive opportunity all the time, and it is distinct from the attitude of **entitlement**.

If you hold an attitude of entitlement, you assume life is going to go a certain way. You will be upset when life comes to you in an unexpected way. You may blame someone or something for what has happened. Most likely, you will see no role in the outcome, which will leave you powerless to create your life. You will be at life's mercy, wishing the situation had occurred differently

If you find you are upset, see if you are holding an attitude of entitlement. How could you be grateful in the same situation? What is there to be thankful for? How would your life be if you were always in gratitude?

Choosing to be grateful allows events in life to be viewed through a positive filter. A grateful person is thankful for the lesson. When a relationship ends, a grateful person is thankful to meet the next person who is to be in his or her life. A grateful person is happy to get caught in a lie so he or she can live a life of integrity.

Being grateful will provide a foundation of noticing what comes your way is of value and is happening to either teach or nurture you. Say "thank you" out loud, even when your initial reaction might be less than grateful.

There is something magical that happens by saying thank you out loud and being grateful; it will shift your focus and you will notice new opportunities in situations.

Another subtlety of gratitude is to be of service. It will keep you feeling equal to other people, as well as balanced on the giver/taker scale.

When I volunteer for different causes, I realize the difference I can make in others' lives. —Steve Knaebel.

Do you feel a need to receive credit for good deeds? If you answered yes, can you refocus yourself to be grateful for the opportunity to be valuable to others? Are you grateful for the capabilities you have?

Practice by being grateful for each moment that comes your way, no matter what the situation. Notice if you feel you deserve something in life. Continue to distinguish being grateful versus being entitled to having things go your way. Do something for someone each day and notice how you feel.

Freedom – choosing an attitude of freedom allows for letting go of expectations in life. How would your life change if you were free to experience life as it occurs, not wishing something or someone was different? How would you be if you trusted everything would work out? How much aliveness could you bring to each moment?

Choosing freedom creates moments filled with joy in your life and is distinct from the attitude of **attachment**.

If you choose an attitude of attachment, you become upset when things turn out different or follow another path than what you invented. You miss what can be created, as you are focused on controlling things to work out as you wanted.

Attachment fills your life with upsets, anger, and relationships that are in conflict.

If you find you are upset, see if you are holding an attitude of attachment. How could you let go and be free to what life offers you? What becomes possible? How would your life be if you were free of attachments?

Choosing freedom allows you to enjoy whatever happens. You can focus your energy solely on what you are committed to creating versus what actually gets created. Think about this for a moment.

38

This leaves you completely powerful to create your life. It allows you to let go of being upset with anything and anyone because your energy stays with what you are committed to create. You are no longer reacting negatively to what gets created.

Instead, you notice what gets created and adjust until what you are committed to gets created. You are now free—what actually gets created only serves as a measure to test your actions and whether they are creating what you are committed to.

When you create this freedom for your life, you have power to generate the life you love. For example, if you were committed to growing your sales organization by twenty percent, you might spend your energy building confidence in your team. You could share best practices in the industry. You could hire a coach to increase the skill of your team. You could put all your energy into actions that would cause your team to increase sales by twenty percent, or you could put all your energy into managing the result of twenty percent growth.

If you spent your energy managing the result, you might spend your time and energy looking at the fact that you have only grown by ten percent. You might yell and scream at your team. You might put in place contests and track them daily on growth towards your goal. You could spend all your energy watching and managing the result, and have little impact on taking actions that could actually create a twenty-percent-growing team.

If you put your energy toward what you are committed to versus managing the results, what opens up for you? For your team? For your family? For your relationships?

To bring this alive in your life, find a situation where you are frustrated. What results have you been expecting? What do you want others to do? Are you spending energy on the results or on actions that might create what you are committed to?

Are your actions consistent with your commitment? Take a moment to understand why others are not following your lead. Demanding others do something and seeing them not play along is frustrating.

39

This frustration generally causes you to try to control things even more. As you might guess, this leads to more frustration.

Controlling comes from the attitude of attachment. The attitude of freedom allows for the possibility of something greater than you envisioned happening.

Occasionally, we all will slip and have expectations about how something should work, look, or happen. We find ourselves disappointed. Sparky people survive disappointment, viewing it as an occasion for learning versus a justification for withdrawal.

I ask myself, what was the gift in this disappointment? What expectation did I create that caused me to be disappointed? What is there for me here? —Gary Hirsch.

Everyone I interviewed had their share of disappointments, as they were guilty of having expectations of results (attachment). It is important to note that the more focused they were on their intention instead of the outcome, the better their lives worked.

So the freer you can be from results, the fewer disappointments you will create in your life.

Practice by putting your entire focus on your actions. Take actions consistent with your intentions and completely let go of controlling the results. Trust the results will be a direct reflection of your actions. Notice when you go into controlling mode and what that creates for yourself and others in your life.

Journey-Orientation – choosing an attitude of journey-orientation allows for engaging in life with a focus on who you are being in the moment instead of what you are accomplishing. If ninety-nine percent of your life is spent on the journey and one percent on the results achieved, which part do you want to make sure you enjoy?

Journey-orientation allows for joy along the entire ride during your life, and it is distinct from the attitude of **task-orientation**.

If you are a task-oriented person, you are driven to complete checklists, to get things done. You receive satisfaction once something is completed. However, you usually only have a brief moment to enjoy because there is something else to get done. You are on to the next task.

Task-oriented people are often financially successful in life, but sometimes they lack satisfaction in their lives. They generally have people in their lives, but they are often too busy to create closeness. This is because it is not one of their tasks to complete.

When I am solely goal-focused, I spend most of my time being anxious about completing my work. —Gary Hirsch.

Choosing to be journey-oriented puts the emphasis on who you are in the moment, not what you are doing and accomplishing. It allows magic to occur along the way because you are more committed to being in the moment than finishing something.

How can joy happen in the midst of living your purpose? If purpose is a lifelong quest, then what is the hurry? This struck me, since I was focused on doing and accomplishing.

When I saw life as just one task—to live my purpose—then I easily let go of hurrying to get things done. The only hurry I had was to consistently be who I was committed to being. That inspired me.

Sparky people know how to find joy during their journeys, finding moments of laughter, fun, and plain silliness during day-to-day activities.

Make your state of mind more important than what you are doing. —Hugh Prather.

Think about that for a minute. In your life, has your state of mind ever been more important than what you were doing?

When someone interrupts you, how do you respond? Is what you are doing so vital that it cannot be interrupted? What do you miss by not allowing interruptions? What do others miss by not being able to interrupt you?

Practice laughing, loving, and smiling during the day-to-day tasks you perform. Notice if you are enjoying the process of being or if you are more focused on what you are doing and accomplishing. Make yourself a joy to be around and gladly let yourself be interrupted.

Fascination – choosing an attitude of fascination is being forever in a state of wonder. It is not knowing the answer.

I'm always fascinated with people and things; they give me unending opportunities to learn —Mechai Viravaldya.

If you choose anything, become fascinated again. This is one of the main reasons young children have incredible spark. Everything is fascinating. **Most people unlearn this natural gift**. Being fascinated is distinct from the attitude of **know-it-all**.

When you have an attitude of know-it-all, you have things figured out before they happen. You have been there, done that, and don't need to experience it again. You know how others will react, what others are capable of, and why things happen. You recognize things quickly and assign an appropriate label to interpret the moment.

When you come from a place of knowing, it creates a constant world full of predictable tasks and predictable people, and with minimal opportunities for learning. Most likely, a knowing person can only learn where they KNOW they can learn. Life holds little surprise or mystery.

Choosing to be fascinated allows the same events in life to be viewed through a filter of possibility. One of the practices taught to me was to learn something new about each thing you think you already know everything about. One example is your best friend. What is something you don't know about her? How does she make decisions? What makes a day memorable for him? What is his favorite season? What is his or her purpose in life?

Can we practice becoming fascinated again? One technique is to break routine.

42

It's not about finding an alternative, it is realizing that there is one!
—Gary Hirsch.

Gary consistently forces himself to break routine, not just to do new things, but also to keep his mind attuned to seeing things differently. The challenge is to avoid judging things as soon as they come at you.

If you have created judgment filters, you will probably assess things quickly. This can cause you to miss something as your judgment filters limit what is possible.

How would it be to experience life from a place of fascination vs. judgment? Breaking routine may make it easier to recognize judgment filters you have created and remove them. Then you can experience new people, familiar people, and new moments with fascination.

Another important facet to being fascinated is retaining your innocence.

Innocent is different than uninformed. It is about greeting each moment unconstrained by the moments before. —Mickey Connolly.

Again, this speaks to removing judgment filters. Don't see things based on past events; allow yourself to experience the situation or person unconstrained by situations or people you have met before. Stay innocent and remain open to what can happen.

Have you had an experience where something turned out completely different than you expected? What if you didn't expect things to turn out a certain way?

People with spark practice living without expectations. Can you stay open to how things will unfold? If you personally stay open, will the world also magically remain open?

Seek always, for by looking for one thing, you will surely find another. But never look and you will never find anything.
—Celtic Proverb.

Practice seeking more from what comes your way. Experience the moment brand new. Resist the urge to know the answer, to look smart. Instead, ask questions about that which you thought you already knew.

At Choice – choosing an attitude of "at choice" gives you power to create your life. You are aware you always have a choice, and you recognize how those choices create what is happening in your life.

I was taught that there is no such thing as can't, only won't, and I was always conscious of the difference —Laura Stepp.

The amazing thing about this quote is the recognition of choice. If you won't do something, it implies making a conscious choice. If you can't do something, it implies an inability and leaves you at the mercy of life. At Choice is distinct from the attitude of **victim**.

When you live with an attitude of victim, you are without power to create your life. Your life is determined by other people and by circumstances beyond your control. Being a victim leads to being upset, disappointed, and without hope of living a life you love.

When you are a victim, you wonder why good things happen to other people. You hope that something great will happen to you. You do not see the link between your choices and how your life is turning out.

Choosing to be at choice allows you to have complete responsibility for your life. If life is not working for you, it is due to the choices you have made. The power therein is that you can make a new choice.

Noticing when you are limiting what is possible in your life requires that you pay attention.

When we're in transition is when the biggest lessons arrive. Don't miss them. Sometimes I get anxious about the change and I miss noticing the choices that I have made and am making. —Aaron Hornstein.

The only opportunity you have to make a new choice starts with noticing that you *have* made a choice.

The challenge to being observant is noticing areas where you are unconsciously walking through life. I am conscious in certain aspects of my life (e.g., how other people are reacting) but unconscious in other areas (e.g., how people need to go through their own process to get somewhere).

The skill is in understanding the choices you have made are completely responsible for what is happening in your life.

If you do what you've always done, you'll get what you always got —unknown source.

Think about this quote for a minute. Do you see the same lesson repeating itself in your life?

The people I interviewed were conscious of choice. It's not that they always made great choices, but they quickly correlated how the choices they made caused what wasn't working in their life.

Practice by selecting the areas in your life where you are stuck or unhappy. Identify the choices that created your situation. Notice if you are blaming anyone or anything for what is going on. Create and act on new choices.

Inclusion – choosing an attitude of inclusion allows for selecting and enrolling others in your journey. How is your purpose enhanced by having collaborators? Inclusiveness is another aspect of spark that surprised me.

Sparky people really want others to join them on the journey, even when it appears the joiners might take business away from their endeavors. People with spark were more committed to their purpose than anything else, so all joiners increased the possibility of success. Being inclusive is distinct from the attitude of **competition**.

A competitive person generally celebrates alone. Getting credit/looking good is of utmost importance, and others often resent them. They are suspicious of others' motives, seeing them as trying to take from the competitive person or being jealous of their abilities.

This creates a life of protecting what is *mine*. Competitive people distance themselves from other people because "they want what I have, they aren't good enough, and they can't be trusted."

Many people get caught up in winning. They often miss out on what they wanted to create in life, which is why they wanted to win in the first place.

Choosing to be inclusive allows others in on your journey. It is important to step back and determine what the ultimate win is. It may be that winning this contract or getting the money for this sale isn't as valuable as increasing the size of the team or increasing your chances to change the world.

It may be that you will gain more business, more friends, and more joy by collaborating and gaining new understandings than by cutting others out.

Does being competitive create allies or enemies? What determines if someone becomes an ally or an enemy? Have you ever created an enemy?

Could an enemy have been turned into an ally at some point? How much of your energy goes into fighting an enemy, and is that energy productive, leading you where you want to go? If you had spent that same energy creating an ally, how would your life be different? How would your enemy's life be different?

Practice enrolling collaborators, especially those you initially saw as competitors. Resist the urge to claim victory. Take a minute to find a win for all parties. Notice what is created for yourself and others when you are inclusive.

Excellence – choosing an attitude of excellence allows for being extremely effective at what you are committed to.

Don't be afraid of being awesome. —Kay Stepp.

Sparky people approach life intending to be incredible. Incredible in how they show up for people. Incredible in how they love others. Incredible in how they show their joy. Incredible in how they laugh and share the moments of life. Incredible in how they go for what matters to them, holding nothing back.

Excellence is more than how you perform a task; it is extending all that is within you. Excellence is distinct from the attitude of **perfection**.

A perfectionist is focused on excellence in just one area. The excellence in that one area is achieved at the cost of other areas.

For example, a teacher who is a perfectionist decides his class will be excellent at drawing trees. He tells his students how to draw trees and scolds them until they draw trees according to his idea of perfection. In this example, perfection is achieved at the cost of fun and confidence. The students don't enjoy drawing, and they don't feel good about their abilities to be great artists.

If the teacher was committed to being excellent (in terms of an attitude that creates spark), then they would have balanced drawing with fun, creativity, and joy.

How often do you choose your perception of perfection over others' enjoyment? What is the cost? What is gained? Is the gain worth the cost?

Choosing to be excellent involves being clear about doing your best while still being the person you want to be. If you find you are a perfectionist, utilize your need to be perfect by redefining what perfect is. Let perfection be "living the most beautiful life." Become perfect at that!

Practice showing up for people and your endeavors with the intention of being incredible. Don't sacrifice anything about who you want to be for task perfection.

Humor – choosing an attitude of humor allows you to be someone that brings laughter into life. Humor relieves pain and allows us to see there are several ways to interpret anything in life.

What does humor open up inside relationships? Where is humor valuable in identifying new choices in life? How can humor create joy for other people?

If we can laugh at ourselves, it is hard to mistake things as so serious. —Martin Goebel.

Humor is distinct from the attitude of **seriousness**.

Serious people can only see things through their points of view. Their time is more valuable than others' time; their issues are more interesting and pressing than others' issues. Their lives are of greater concern. They have little time for those who don't fit into what they are doing.

Choosing to be humorous allows a person to laugh about himself and realize he is just like everyone else, no better and no worse. Humor creates an opportunity to enjoy failure, so we put ourselves in the game of life more often.

When life is serious and significant, how do you show up? Are you effective? Is there an alternative? Can you use humor?

Being able to enjoy the journey requires laughter during setbacks and failures. Laughing and seeing the joy of life creates space for mistakes, failures, lessons, forgiveness, and for being human. None of this is possible if it is so significant.

If you keep things serious, what do you miss? In a recent study, the results showed that the average preschooler laughs 350 times a day, while the average adult only laughs 10 times a day.

Are you closer to the average adult or the average preschooler? If you don't laugh, what happens to your experience? Does it cause you to be more serious? If you laugh, what does it cause? How do you trap yourself in serious situations where laughter is not acceptable? Could you be more effective if you committed to an attitude of humor?

Practice finding the humor in a serious situation. See if you can lighten your view during a tense time. If something seems incredibly important to you, notice what place it will have in your life five years from now. Does that open a new possibility for you?

Passion – choosing an attitude of passion means being someone who cares deeply about what is happening in life. When you allow yourself to be passionate about people and your endeavors, your mind focuses on the possibilities. You increase your resolve to go through barriers.

Can you be passionate about your purpose and not get attached to how things look or what path it will take to get there? Can you be passionate and still retain your humor?

Passion is distinct from the attitude of **withdrawal**.

When you withdraw from what you want to accomplish in life, you lose power. You undermine your confidence. Sometimes this is caused by impatience and the expectation that what you are up to should happen immediately. Sometimes this is caused by not understanding the correlation between actions and results—expecting results with little action.

No matter what leads to withdrawal, it brings a resignation to your life. If you begin to give up, how willing are you to take part the next time? Do you spend energy justifying why things don't matter, why they are not important, and why you are not participating?

How do you feel around people who are withdrawn? Are you compelled to spend time with them, join them, or get involved in their life?

Choosing to be passionate calls you to cause something in the world. You have a drive to figure your way through obstacles and over hurdles. Your commitment is contagious and can draw others to your cause.

Notice that it is possible to be passionate without sacrificing who you want to be in life. Passion only speaks to your commitment level. It does not imply you are serious or attached to the results.

When you have felt intensely passionate about something, what happened? Conversely, when you distance yourself from people and endeavors, how do you feel about them? What do you risk by becoming passionate? What do you sacrifice by not being passionate?

Practice loving something in every person you greet. Search for what is brilliant about them. Involve all of yourself in your actions. Unleash your passion.

Confidence – choosing an attitude of confidence creates certainty in your ability to be who you are committed to being and to take action in the world. Action is a key component in being confident. When you are truly confident, you risk failure. You are confident you will find your way in life.

Risk is stimulating and standing for anything in life requires it. When you risk, you break through fear barriers, and from that moment on, your comfort zone is forever stretched. Taking risks allows you to do more and more, moving through fears and building confidence.

Confidence is created both by realizing things are not as scary as we think they are and by developing skills. Confidence is distinct from the attitude of **uncertainty**.

When you are uncertain, you spend time thinking instead of taking actions. You pretend to be moving toward action by analyzing, preparing, and performing due diligence. But you rarely move to action, so you don't actually cause anything to happen. You miss out on the excitement caused by putting yourself into a position where you could succeed because you are so afraid of failing or looking bad.

When you have confidence, you continue to create in life. You are not stopped by failure along the way. You learn to adapt and find success through the teachings from your failures.

If you are uncertain, you miss the experience gained from failure. You do not create that learning in your life.

That which I fear, I know I must do. —Eleanor Roosevelt.

When you are confident, you believe change is possible despite the evidence. You focus on possibilities, asking, "How could this work?"

There is always evidence that something is impossible, so it takes a confident person to see beyond the practical for new proof to make it into the world.

The reasonable man adapts himself to the world, while the unreasonable man adapts the world to himself. Therefore, all progress depends on the unreasonable man. —George Bernard Shaw.

Nothing new will ever happen if you don't remain hopeful in spite of the evidence. Notice if the joy of taking risks that pay off outweighs the consequence of risks that don't. Also, notice how you change as a result of taking risks.

Does fear of failure keep you from living? What if you embrace failure as learning? Would you risk more? Notice if you spend time analyzing as a stalling tactic.

Practice taking risks in your dealings with people, in your job, and in your life. Notice what changes. How does confidence affect your spark?

Now, let's work on some exercises to understand your attitudes as they exist and how new attitudes might serve your purpose.

1) Expose your existing attitudes. What are your existing attitudes? Do you know how they affect your experience of life? Are there any attitudes that limit you?

Let's identify potential attitudes and understand how they affect your experience of living. Answer the following questions with the first Yes/No answer that comes to mind. This exercise is for you. You do not have to show anyone your answers. Be completely honest, even if you don't like your answer. Don't judge as you write. We'll review it together as we study how it affects your experience in living this life.

- When you do something, do you seek credit?
- When things go wrong, do you get frustrated quickly?
- Do you avoid volunteering to help others, instead waiting to be asked?

Let's examine your answers. If you answered yes to any of the questions above, you may have an attitude that people and the world owe you and that things should turn out to satisfy you (entitlement). If this holds any truth, then think about how this attitude affects your life. How does this affect how you approach people, volunteer, and help others when they need you? How does this disable you from seeing a bigger picture and other possibilities in life? Where is your focus?

The suggested attitude is **Gratitude**. Be grateful that you had the opportunity to do something and learn from it (e.g., no need for credit). Be grateful that when something goes wrong, you have a chance to change it and learn to do it better for all future attempts (versus being frustrated). Be grateful to have a friend who needs help moving (e.g., is it annoying to spend a Saturday helping a friend move?).

- When you have something to do, is the majority of your sat-isfaction from completing the task?
- If others are involved, do you like them to do things a cer-tain way?
- If life turns out completely different than you expected, are you frustrated?

Let's examine your answers. If you answered yes to any of the questions above, you may have an attitude of being best served by con-trolling how things go (attachment). If this holds any truth, then think about how this attitude affects your life. How does this affect how you manage projects, spend time with your kids, and lead group discussions? How does this disable you from seeing other people's ideas and solutions? How do others feel around you?

The suggested attitude is **_Freedom_**. Be free from controlling results so you can focus on the joy of being (e.g., not just happy when the work is finished). Be free from controlling how others do their work so you can enjoy their creative approaches and learn from them (Can it still go well if it isn't your way?). Be free from what the finished effort looks like, so you can notice a potentially greater learning or endpoint (e.g., the endpoint may open a completely different possibility than you had envisioned, and that could be a great thing).

- When you are driving, does it bother you if someone in the car needs to stop on the way?
- When you are focused on a project and it is important, does it annoy you if someone wants to help (e.g., a child)?
- Do you view doing laundry, going to work, and walking the dog as chores?

Let's examine your answers. If you answered yes to any of the questions above, you may have an attitude that life is to be savored when tasks are completed (task-orientation). If this holds any truth, then think about how this attitude affects your life. How does this affect how you share important projects? How does this disable you from wanting to include people? When mistakes or errors occur, how do you react? Who receives your reaction? Do people want to join you?

The suggested attitude is **_Journey-Orientation_**. Be journey-oriented and enjoy the trip while it happens, not after it has occurred (e.g., don't be in a hurry for life to be complete; ninety-nine percent of life is in the traveling, and only one percent in arriving at the destination). Be journey-oriented and realize that someone else working with you creates a bonding and learning opportunity (e.g., could that be more meaningful than getting the project finished?). Be journey-oriented and enjoy the day-to-day moments of life, figuring out how to make them fun (versus to-dos that get checked off as complete).

- When you are in a situation where you have experience, are you likely to jump in front with your knowledge (e.g., I know the answer)?
- Do you form opinions of other people before you have talked to them?
- If someone suggests a change to your plan, are you annoyed?

Let's examine your answers. If you answered yes to any of the questions above, you may have an attitude that you know the answer given the circumstances (Know-It-All). If this holds any truth, think about how this attitude affects your life. How does this affect how you size up people you are meeting? How does this disable you from seeing someone else's point of view? How does this affect your being open to another possibility?

The suggested attitude is **Fascinated**. Be fascinated to learn more about the situation, finding out what might be different or new (e.g., not knowing the answer and wanting to tell others). Be fascinated to understand how this person ticks, what matters to them, what they are afraid of, etc. (versus figuring them out based on some quick judgments). Be fascinated to understand why they want to change the plan (e.g., it may not have anything to do with you).

- Do things happen to you?
- Are you at a disadvantage because others have more than you?
- Do people ignore your needs?

Let's examine your answers. If you answered yes to any of the questions above, you may have an attitude that life happens to you (victim). If this holds any truth, think about how this attitude affects your life. How does this affect how you see choices available to you? How does this disable you from seeing your responsibility in your life? How does this cause you to relate to other people in the world?

The suggested attitude is **At Choice**. Be at choice so you can choose different surroundings, new people, etc., so things don't happen to you (e.g., understand your role in creating the situation). Be at choice so you can change your current situation so you are not disadvantaged (remove the excuse that keeps you stuck). Be at choice so you can take responsibility for your own needs and satisfy them (e.g., see your role in putting someone in a role to fill your needs).

- Do you see other capable people as threats to take your projects, your friends, or your clients?
- Do you want to show others you are smarter, more skilled, or more experienced?
- Do you like to do the cool projects yourself?

Let's examine your answers. If you answered yes to any of the questions above, you may have an attitude that you must compete in life to get what you want (competition). If this holds any truth, then think about how this attitude affects your life. How does this affect how you involve others? How does this disable you from creating greater capability in the world? Does this allow your world to grow bigger? How will this affect anothers desire to share with you? Does this cultivate trust? Will others be drawn to you?

The suggested attitude is **Inclusion**. Be inclusive by sharing good projects, introducing others to your clients, etc., so that your world becomes bigger (e.g., more people will want to share with you). Be inclusive and let others shine and demonstrate their special gifts (people will look to you as a leader). Be inclusive and allow others to gain experience on the cool projects (e.g., you would increase the overall team ability to do complex, engaging work, thinking like a leader).

- If you know you can win the game, is it okay for the team to be in conflict?
- Do you hold your child to a higher standard than they hold themselves?
- At work, are you more committed to getting it done right than being who you want to be?

Let's examine your answers. If you answered yes to any of the questions above, you may have an attitude that a task has to be done a certain way (perfection). If this holds any truth, then think about how this attitude affects your life. How does this affect how others feel about you? How does this cause you to show up with those you care about? How do others show up for you? Are people or tasks more important in your life?

The suggested attitude is **Excellence**. Be excellent and create a win for everyone (e.g., create a great experience that brings everyone together). Be excellent and create an opportunity for your child to learn how incredible they are and how much you appreciate their help (take time to be about people not just completion). Be excellent and show up as who you want to be first and foremost.

If something really matters to you, do you find that you become serious automatically?

55

When you have setbacks, is your first reaction one of annoyance? Does it make you upset if someone laughs at one of your mistakes?

Let's examine your answers. If you answered yes to any of the questions above, you may have an attitude that when things matter, being serious about them is most effective (seriousness). If this holds any truth, think about how this attitude affects your life. How does this affect how much you enjoy yourself? How does this affect how much fun others have with you? How will this affect your ability to see other possibilities? What atmosphere do you create? What price do others pay to join you on important projects? How are you being with your team?

The suggested attitude is **Humor**. Be humorous and create a space for new ideas and more lighthearted disagreement (e.g., you are open to laughing about serious topics). Be humorous and laugh at setbacks. Create an atmosphere that it is okay to fail (e.g., it is okay to take risks). Be humorous and laugh at yourself and give others permission to critique your decisions and what choices you have made (e.g., it opens the space for disagreement in a comfortable atmosphere).

- If something does not go your way, do you pretend not to care anymore?
- Do you look for others to commit to something before making your decision?
- Over time, do you typically enjoy a person less as you get to know them better?

Let's examine your answers. If you answered yes to any of the questions above, you may have an attitude that you don't want to play unless you know it will work out (withdrawal). If this holds any truth, think about how this attitude affects your life. How might this affect your leadership? How will this affect your ability to go after what you really want? What does this cause you to miss? What price do others pay if they don't say yes to you?

The suggested attitude is **Passion**. Be passionate and continue on your journey despite setbacks (e.g., find ways to keep going). Be passionate and take the lead on what matters to you regardless of others' interests (e.g., determine what matters to you, commit, and go for it). Be passionate and find new and exciting things about others; keep learning about them (e.g., give yourself reasons to get closer to someone versus reasons to withdraw).

- When faced with an important decision, do you ask several people's opinion?
- Do you have several decisions that you are waiting to make?
- Are you embarrassed if you fail?

Let's examine your answers. If you answered yes to any of the questions above, you may have an attitude that getting it right before you take action is critical (uncertainty). If this holds any truth, think about how this attitude affects your life. How does this affect your relationships? How effective are you at taking action? How does this affect your level of excitement? What atmosphere do you create with regard to taking risks? What are you reinforcing to yourself and others?

The suggested attitude is **_Confidence_**. Be confident and know you will learn by taking action (do you learn more by watching others or by experiencing life?). Be confident and make a decision, knowing if it is a decision that doesn't work, you will notice and make a new decision. Be confident and know that failure is okay and part of the process of learning quickly and gaining success (e.g., failure is not forbidden or even unexpected; it just means you are one step closer to finding success).

2) Practice choosing a sparky attitude. Take the note cards provided about each attitude/approach to life. *You will find the note cards at the end of the book.* Start with the top of the pile and focus on one attitude each day. It is important to incorporate this attitude regularly throughout the day; otherwise you will likely miss opportunities to apply it, unconsciously falling back into old attitudes.

Make a conscious effort to put the note card and attitude where you will see it all day, having constant opportunities to apply it. This may be on your bathroom mirror, on your computer at work, or on the back of your cell phone. At the end of the day, write down in your workbook what happened.

Notice if your day was somehow different than usual, how people responded to you, and how you responded to others. Make comments on what you noticed.

Do this each day with a different note card until you have completed the stack. If you want to increase your spark, start over with the stack when you have finished. Do it again and again until these new attitudes become a conscious part of your daily approach to life. Studies suggest that it takes twenty-one days on average to change an attitude.

How does your attitude/approach affect your purpose? Does it apply more to your Purposeful Self, your Purposeful Calling, or your Purposeful Endeavors? Write down your thoughts in your workbook. Which attitudes are most difficult for you to incorporate? Why? Write down your answer.

Powerful grounding questions:
Does an effective leader behave this way? How do other people get to experience me? How am I being right now? Would I enjoy being with me right now? What other ways could I show up in this moment?

Signs of excellence:
You will see the world as unlimited and full of **magical** opportunities to do anything you set your mind to. You will feel unstoppable. You will notice people appear much more beautiful and capable because you have become that yourself.

People will want to be around you. They will approach you more often for thoughts, advice, and friendship.

You will see opportunities in everything, and your natural inclination will be to be curious.

You will notice your smile is worn often, and you are constantly inspired by other people and their accomplishments. Your life will feel full of possibility.

It is so important to live in the present, as it is the only time you can affect, have an impact, change the world, make someone's day, etc. It is what is real. The present is where factual life is being created. The best you can do is simply be part of it.

Chapter 3 - Immediacy

Yesterday cannot be redone, and tomorrow may look completely different than we imagine, but we can affect today.
—Mrs. Pinkston, my childhood neighbor

Definition:
Immediacy is defined as living right NOW! Your mind, body, eyes, and (yes) everything are engaged with what is happening right now. This may indeed be a giant challenge for everyone, including the author of this book. The happiest people spend their time living in the present, not being preoccupied with the past, fantasizing about the future, wondering what someone meant by their last comment, or thinking about early retirement.

Living outside the present is perhaps the biggest problem facing society today. It cannot be overstated.

It causes us to start wars because of anticipated futures that may never occur. It causes us to hold grudges because of something that happened yesterday. It causes us to be anxious, nervous, and worried about events that may never happen. It causes us to hold onto being angry, hurt, upset, and sad because of something that cannot be changed.

What would life be like if you only focused on the moment? How would you feel about yourself if you took action right now instead of worrying about it? What if you forgave people right now instead of holding onto hurt? What if you spent the majority of your thoughts on things you were going to do now? How might your life be different?

Would you feel more capable? Could you affect your situation? Would you feel powerful? Would you spend more time in action and less time thinking? Would you have the time to create the life you love?

How living with Immediacy affects spark:
It is so important to live in the present, as it is the only time you can affect, have an impact, change the world, make someone's day, etc. It is what is real. The present is where factual life is being created. The best you can do is simply be part of it.

It is your choice to notice how much time you spend living somewhere other than NOW, and it is also your choice to change the mixture. Ask yourself, is the present moment lacking anything? What is missing? Is everything available to you right now? If you believe that it is, what choices will you make NOW?

When you spend your life living out events that happened yesterday, you sacrifice what is available to be created today.

Energy spent creating life is renewing and invigorating. Energy spent analyzing something that cannot be changed or worrying about something that might never happen is draining. The more time spent analyzing and reanalyzing or worrying, the more energy you lose. However, the more time you spend taking action and creating the life you love, the more energy you will have!

If you spend your time taking action to create the life you love, how would your level of spark be affected? What would happen to the past disappointments? What would happen to future worries?

If you have low energy levels, pay attention to whether you are living in the past (upset about something that cannot be changed) or in the future (worrying about an event that may not even happen).

Remember, noticing our choices and taking action on them right now allows us to create our lives. If you can master identifying when you are being past- or future-oriented by noticing your energy level, you can free yourself to spend your life living in the present.

How noticing where you spend energy can bring you back to living NOW:

Terri Watson, Pilot and Eccentric Adventurer

Terri grew up in Wyoming, spending endless summers splashing in the pool and relaxing at her grandparents' home. She loved to swim and the days seemed to last forever. It was a magical time being a child. Terri remembers being incredibly joyful; worrying was not part of her life.

High school seemed to change this for Terri.

"I started worrying about what other people thought of me. I worried if they liked what I wore, if I was good looking enough, or if I was a good dancer. I doubted myself for the first time."

When do you worry? How does worrying take you out of living in the present?

When Terri started to travel overseas for school she saw how diverse the world was and it struck her that nothing was certain.

Terri realized that when she was not sure about things, she worried. She devised solutions for potential problems that had not yet come to pass. Sometimes it was about fear, and sometimes it was about not being "enough."

"I was always thinking of what was coming next, or of what I did wrong in the past. I never just sat still and enjoyed where I was because I was always focused elsewhere."

Is worrying a solution to uncertainty? Does worrying help you make choices that enable living a life you love?

Most of us worry about what other people think, about what could happen in the world, and about what could happen to us. Our news stations, magazines, advertisements, and schools all feed our worries.

I don't underestimate the challenge of living NOW. To make it easier, we need to choose what supports us. In the chapter on environment, we will talk about setting ourselves up to succeed.

After college, Terri went into the military. While finding great success in her flying, she spent her entire time focused on the next thing to do. She worried about aircraft training school, her next assignment, and her next promotion.

"I was never where I needed to be. There was always something more I needed to do in order to become the someone I wanted to be."

Do you spend energy doing something in order to become something? Is it necessary to do anything in order to become who you want to be? Who created the tie between doing and being?

Leaving military service, Terri worked in an outdoor school in Baja, Mexico, for several months each year. She would take students sea kayaking or sailing for four weeks at a time. They would travel, camp, swim, and learn the skills needed to travel safely and comfortably in the wilderness. Terri remembers she was the envy of all her friends, who thought her life was amazing.

But Terri wasn't happy. She was constantly fretting about the what-ifs of life.

"I worried about what the next set of students would be like. I worried about the weather, if we would have the right surf, if I would get along with my coworkers, etc. I could not turn it off. I was the epitome of not living in the NOW!"

It is amazing to notice what happened. Here Terri was in place to have the most magnificent life, but she wasn't happy. What was missing, and was it available in that moment? How could she have tapped into it? How can you see that everything is available in your moments?

Terri used to think that there was a "right" choice, and that if she made the "wrong" choice, there would be all kinds of irreparable repercussions. A lot of angst went into each decision. Even the decision to leave the service was excruciating. She feared ruining her life.

Terri was now thirty and living in fear. She was making decisions based on what she was afraid would happen. Drinking became a real issue. She hoped the fears would go away and she could get by. Instead of living a life she loved, she had settled for finding a tolerable life where she didn't have to worry.

Take a moment to see what choices you are avoiding. What worries you? What fears play in your life? How does fear control you? Have you settled for a tolerable life?

Eventually a car wreck pulled Terri up and caused her to examine life. She approached one of her closest friends and asked for help. Soon, she joined Alcoholics Anonymous (AA) and started the twelve-step process. She learned she had no control over anything outside herself.

To live in the NOW, Terri uses the image of hiking on a rugged trail. She learned to spend most of her time seeing where to place her feet (the present). Sometimes the path would not be smooth, but the focus was simply making the next step a solid one. Every so often she glances up to make sure she knows where she's going (the future), and she looks back once in awhile to make sure she learns from where she's been (the past).

This balance has been crucial to her enjoying life again. If Terri has a hard day, she focuses on what is in the here and now, what is the very next decision that needs to be made in this moment. It might be as simple as where she is going to get her coffee or which row of cars to turn up to find a parking place.

The discipline of not letting herself run ahead and worry about the what-ifs later in the day keeps her focused on the moment.

Terri notices now when she starts spinning or feeling out of sorts; she hears herself using fear words.

"I pay attention to myself, and if I hear myself say things like, 'I'm afraid that' then I pull myself back. Recently, I was figuring out how I was going to take on my insurance company and going down a trail of how to convince them, creating a game plan if it went to court, and they had not even denied the claim!" laughs Terri.

How might you notice when you are worrying or upset? How can you pull yourself back to choosing actions available right now?

Terri found that once she admitted a lack of control over people, places, and things outside herself, she stopped spending time trying to exert influence where she had none. She believes having a spiritual base is important to living in the now, whether that be God, the Universe, Buddha, or some other greater force.

"I have to let go of trying to control other things, and trust my higher power to take care of those things."

Terri ends with describing how her love life, her family life, and her career are all at high points. "It's not that suddenly everything is working out and good things have finally come, it's that I am finally truly happy with how things are, no matter what, and open to what is going to come next. When I am happy in the moment, living in the now, everything is good."

Terri once again is enjoying the moments as they come.

How choosing your perspective can bring you back to living NOW:

Lori Wisbeck, Mother, Wife, PacifiCorp Employee, and Cancer Patient

Lori doesn't think she learned to live in the NOW until her first diagnosis with cancer. "I didn't know what it was until then. Everything became important."

Once she was in remission, Lori fell out of the moment again. "I didn't know I was falling out of living in the moment. I lost track and started taking life for granted again. I worried about money and status. It gradually crept back in. I thought I had grasped what living in the moment was, but I didn't really know."

How does wanting something cause you to live in the future? The experience of wanting takes our focus off creating. Creating requires action NOW, while wanting leaves us with a feeling of lacking something.

Lori was re-diagnosed with cancer, which sent her back into living in the moment. "Every learning experience became important. I was grasping to be here, and I went to the extreme, trying to live every single moment. I learned that you don't grab it all at once or you become overwhelmed, and then you are not in the moment anymore. I was so frustrated and afraid that I wouldn't be able to do everything and learn everything I wanted to and that I would leave this life unfulfilled."

Lori decided to take a step back and rather than grasp at it all, she decided to live each day being peaceful. She decided she could not be perfect.

"I see all these people, and they want this perfect life. I know I did. Now, I let things fall into place. It's not that I don't want things or even that I don't get caught up in making things look a certain way, but when I am in the moment, I let things fall into place. I live and I don't think ahead. I also don't worry if things don't happen."

How can taking actions now create your world? How would that be different than wanting something else in your life?

Lori had a friend come out to *Race for the Cure*. They decided to take action and make a difference in fighting cancer.

"I wasn't worried about the before or after. I didn't think about what I did in the morning or what I was going to do that night. I just soaked it all up, the whole race, even the pain. It was great."

Lori is back on chemotherapy and does what she can each day. Living in the moment is now part of her natural thinking.

"I don't even think about living in the moment. I just do. It's not always joyful; there is pain and sorrow. But I get through without mulling it over and staying focused on it. Life is about going with the flow."

Lori feels the key to contentment is accepting life and what God has given her. She doesn't ask for more. "You can seek out more and want more. More of *what* I am not sure—happiness, possessions—it is beyond me. When I want contentment, I don't find it."

Lori's nurse occasionally refocuses her if she gets that deer-in-the-headlights look. She helps Lori decide if this is the final phase of a journey or a new step on her next journey. "She helps me to accept what life brings and enjoy the ones that I love. I know the tumors in my liver won't go away. Cancer and I live together. I have accepted this journey, and I go day to day, creating what I can."

Lori hopes those close to her will someday walk with her. She knows it is hard for them, as they want the cancer to go away. They want a magical cure.

"In a way, everyone has a terminal illness. Each minute we are that much closer to death. I think it is a mistake to deny the finiteness of life. I say enjoy your time now, whatever that is."

Lori believes in many ways it is a blessing to know the license plate of the bus that is going to kill you. She knows her fate, and that takes the fear out of it.

"I know the end of the story; I just don't know how I am going to get there! That is what I get to create each day."

Last Memorial Day weekend, Lori went to Wallowa Lake. "That was big. It was a breathtaking experience with great friends. I not only saw the picture, but I got to become part of the picture."

Another moment was at Man Lake. At midnight, the wind blew so hard the tent fell over on them and they thought they were going to roll into the lake. "We were so dirty. That was not one of my better moments," she laughs.

Lori thinks the best memories are when you really laugh or really cry, and hopefully you learn from the sad moments and become a better person.

How does Lori's perspective of creating versus wanting keep her living in the moment? How does it give her power in her life?

"If my husband or my mother accepted my cancer rather than wanting it to be gone, they would find it's a lot easier to live. Their hearts would not be so heavy. When you want something to be different, you spend all this time creating falseness and not living. Energy is spent on not telling the truth. Even if the truth is painful, the consequences of denial are worse. When you are honest with yourself, it opens the doors to living!"

Lori doesn't deny thoughts, feelings, or events that happen in her life. When things go wrong, she has learned not to worry about what happened or how it looked, since stress negatively affects her immune system.

How is Lori's acceptance of her life a pathway to creating the life she wants? How would Lori's life be different if she wanted to be free of cancer? How could your acceptance of your life be a pathway to creating the life you want? How would wanting your life to be different affect your ability to create the life you love?

For Lori, another lesson learned is that control is a lost cause. As a teen, Lori wanted to control what others thought about her. As an adult, Lori wanted to be in control of her destiny, but cancer showed up. When she went into remission, Lori sensed renewed control of her destiny and again became complacent with life.

"The biggest lie is if we control our destiny then we get what we expect in life."

Lori's wish for everyone is to not wait to start living. "I hope people don't have to get an illness to feel like I do now; it is so wonderful to be present and live from moment to moment. I have confidence that the time I have left is enough."

How can you stay focused on living in the present?
One of the greatest gifts I received was reading two books: *Taming Your Gremlin* by Richard Carson and *The Power of Now* by Eckhart Tolle. They talked about consciously separating your true self from that voice in your head that wants to engage in analyzing the past or fantasizing about the future, both of which are not reality.

The only reality is what is happening now; the rest is interpretation or fantasy. By becoming conscious, I was able to choose when to analyze and how much time to allow before getting back to what was happening in the moment that I was missing. It really is a choice to obsess about something or to be alive right now.

It is a gift to give yourself joy along the journey. If ninety-nine percent of your time involves going somewhere or accomplishing something (e.g., the journey), and only one percent is the arrival or realization of the achievement (e.g., the result), which part do you want to enjoy?

By learning to enjoy the day-to-day journey, with all of its ups and downs, confusion, indecision, tricks, curves, etc., you can bring your life alive! This is tricky for many people, because they are task-focused.

When did this happen? Do children seem task-focused or journey-focused? What causes adults to become task-focused? What do adults buy into? Is meaning created by what we complete or by how we live? Which is your focus?

Task-focused people generally only enjoy themselves once the task is satisfactorily completed.

Multi-taskers are especially at risk of having little joy. Multi-tasking was invented to get more done in less time, focusing entirely on completion and squeezing efficiency out of time. This concept not only has to be questioned regarding its true efficiency, but also in terms of how much joy is lost by applying it.

The next time you find yourself multi-tasking, notice how present you are in anything going on. Are you half into a conversation on the

70

phone and half into something on the computer, not really enjoying either? How do you feel when other people are multi-tasking while talking to you? Is it obvious when you are talking to a multi-tasker? Do you think you get away with it?

Can you alter task-focus to become journey-focused? If you focus on enjoying the experience, then is the outcome a prerequisite to enjoying yourself? What about the other way around? If you focus on enjoying the outcome, is a joyful experience a prerequisite?

Do children enjoy the experience of playing or the satisfaction of having played effectively? Do you enjoy the experience of life or having completed life effectively?

Gary Hirsch, cofounder of On Your Feet, an improvisational approach to business, took me through an exercise to understand whether it is easier to live anticipating life or reacting to life as it occurs. The exercise involved five objects. In the first exercise:

- Gary placed the objects behind me
- Asked me to back up to the object
- Guess what the object was without looking down
- Incorporate the object into a story
- Then look at what the object actually was
- Change the story if I guessed wrong
- Then back up to the next object
- And do the same thing.

I guessed right on two of the five objects, so I had to change my story sixty percent of the time. For the second exercise, he had me do the same process, but instead of anticipating or guessing what the object was, he had me just look down and incorporate the actual object into the story.

He then asked which I found easier. Of course, looking down and seeing the actual object was much easier. Gary explained that this is how **most people live** their lives, **anticipating** what is going to happen, creating a story around that, then adjusting the story once reality actually happens or bending reality to match what the story was.

Do you anticipate life or live it as it happens? What would it take for you to live life as it happens?

It takes practice to stop anticipating life, so be patient with the process, but be committed. Anticipating life is a much harder life. Consider choosing easy.

If you have been spending a majority of your time in the past or future, it will mean unlearning habits and learning new practices. It will mean becoming conscious and noticing where you are wanting in your life, where you are trying to control your life, and where you are obsessing about something that cannot be undone.

If you can live your purpose moment to moment as uncovered in the first chapter, possess an attitude of seeing the gifts in life as promoted in the second chapter, and focus on creating your life in the moment as discussed in this chapter, you can be present NOW!

Recognize worry; it is a fear state and is about the future, not NOW. Fear is completely about future thinking even though it starts from what has happened in the past. So, let's get started. The first exercise is to recognize past or future-oriented habits.

1) Identify your past- or future-oriented habits. Take out your workbook and write down what habits are big takers of your time. Review the list below and think of additional habits not listed.

- Fears about life, career, relationships, family, death, money, possessions

- Daydreaming

- Replaying conversations/events

- Talking to friends about other friends and what happened

- Wishing for events/things (lottery, retirement, possessions)

- Regretting decisions
- Analyzing/Having conversations in your head with your-self/others
- Abundant planning of future events, meals, trips
- Waiting for the weekend, for a special day, or for someone to get home
- Worrying about some work event, relationship, friend
- Anticipating potential outcomes of conversations, decisions, or events, and planning what you will do if different scenarios happen
- Creating stories about how your life, relationships, or career will play out
- Other habits: take time to think about where you spend a lot of time, and write these down.

While many of these tasks could be enriching to your life, it is good to be aware how much time is spent in the past or future and to notice how much is spent living with what is going on right now. If there are approximately sixteen waking hours each day, how many of those hours do you spend in the above past/future thinking? Try to calculate a number.

Comment on the time spent in these habits and how it affects your present (NOW) focus. How would your life be different if you spent that time focused in the moment? How would it affect your energy level?

Write down how much time you want to commit to past/future-oriented thinking

2) Separate your identity from your mind. Understand that your mind is a tool to be used and ignored as you wish, just like your eyes. Sometimes you direct your eyes to see things, and other times they focus in on things when you aren't consciously directing them. Your mind behaves the same way. It is useful when you consciously direct it to solve a problem or think through a scenario. It can be very destructive when it obsesses about things you aren't consciously directing it to do.

The mind is the single biggest reason most people don't live in the NOW, so gaining control over your mind is tantamount to living in the present moment.

The process is simple. Look at it as a tool to assist you in breaking one of the toughest opponents to living in the present.

Detach yourself from your mind. Witness your mind and what it is thinking about, not owning it as you, but rather observing it like you would another person. You don't own what it is thinking about, you just notice if you want to engage or keep your distance.

Once you have separated yourself and your identity from your mind, it takes its rightful place as a tool at your disposal. So let's practice:

- Notice what you are thinking, and just observe it, setting your mind's thoughts as separate from you. This is available to you at any moment, and this separation allows you to choose when to ignore your mind and when to engage it. Your ability in this area holds the key to your living in the NOW.

  Write down in your workbook everything your mind is think ing about. Resist any connection to it. Rather, just observe your mind and watch it go. Write until it stops or for about fifteen minutes.

  What did you notice? What does your mind like to do?

- Now, allow your mind to continue, but choose to observe something else.

  Explore outside, notice your breathing, or anything right in front of you. Get outside and say hello to everyone you pass. Regardless of what your mind is doing, focus on what is right in front of you.

Observe the buildings, trees, and sky. Notice things you haven't seen before. Do something silly (skip a few steps, sing out loud, whistle, rap) whatever makes you laugh a little bit, and puts you fully in the present moment.

Did you notice where your mind was, while consciously choosing to observe things like your breathing? Did your mind wander off? Where did it wander? Were you able to separate yourself from what your mind was doing? Were you able to direct your mind to focus on what you wanted it to?

Can you see your mind as separate from yourself? Can you see it as a tool that can be used to keep you present or allowed to keep you past/future-focused?

Now, write down what that experience was like. Notice what was the same, what was different, and comment. Notice your perception of time during this exercise. Comment.

If you have been successful at separating your mind from yourself, then answer the following question: At a high level, what do you want? Is it different than what your mind often focuses on? Comment.

3) Separate from past events. It is impossible to be unhappy if you are in the moment, true or false?

I would argue this statement to be true, as the only thing that could make you unhappy is your choice to bring past events into your NOW. Think about that for a minute. Can you be unhappy if you are truly in this moment? Whatever happened, had to occur in the past, correct?

Recognize this as a choice, and make a decision about how to handle the situation or check to see if you are being your Purposeful Self right NOW. Is it possible to keep your past from dictating your NOW? What would that require? Could it be simple?

Does your mind hold onto things that keep you unhappy? Do you indulge your mind by engaging in what it holds onto?

Your life is happening right now. Can that be completely different from what your mind holds onto? Let's practice:

- Where do you have unhappiness or distress in your life?

  Write this down in your workbook. Write every occurrence.

- Can you make an actionable decision in each case? How would the situation alter if you took action? How would you feel? How would resolving these areas affect your ability to live in the present? How would resolution enhance your ability to live a life you love?

  Take a moment to write your answers in your workbook.

The practice is to notice unhappiness or distress of any kind in your life, make a decision on how to deal with the situation, and leave it as done. Be resolved that your decision dealt with it as best you could, and refocus on what is happening right NOW.

- It really is that simple, but it may take some practice to believe it. If you find there is nothing you can do to deal with the situation, then leave it, as you just noticed there is nothing you can do.

- Observe how your mind wants to keep mulling it over. Practice seeing your mind as separate from yourself. Leave space for joy.

- Practice experiencing life as it happens, perhaps differently than what your mind holds. Notice what your mind holds onto and how you used to let that hold you captive in the past or in waiting for the future. This is a key distinction and important to living NOW.

  Write down what you notice happening and your results in choosing to stay separate from your mind.

4) Put it to a test. Spend the remainder of the day separating from your mind.

Stay present and accounted for in the moment. This means:

- Eliminating multi-tasking

- Focusing on who is talking to you (phone or in person)
- Observing the latest drama that your mind wants to dissect and discuss over and over

It is best to use some device to remind you (e.g., a ring, rubber band, or note on your hand). Put it somewhere that you will see it all day long, and have that be your NOW reminder. Don't indulge your mind, observe it!

At the end of the day, write down in your workbook what the experience brought. Notice what was the same and what was different. Notice if this was difficult or easy. If it was difficult, what would make it easier? Write down your answer. How did your mind serve as a tool for you? Did your mind control you? Explain.

Powerful grounding questions:
Where is my mind focused? Is it where I want to be focused? Is everything available to me right now? Who am I committed to being? Am I completely available to what is happening right now? What choice is calling me into action?

Signs of excellence:
The best sign you are living in the NOW is when you are engaged in what is happening in front of you. You are not thinking about something else, somewhere else, or someone else.

You'll feel like you have more time, as more living actually happens in each day. People will notice how present and engaged you are, and they will tell you.

The world will seem bigger. You will feel like you can do more, see more, and experience more in your life. You will notice your energy level is huge, your mood light and positive.

You will be happy and joyful, free to deal with life right as it happens, and you will know the power of that choice.

As much as creation keeps possibility alive, judgment and fear kill it off.

Chapter 4 - Possibility

If you think you can do a thing or think you can't do a thing, you are right. —Henry Ford

Definition:
In terms of spark, possibility speaks to the freedom of your mind. Can you think without limitations?

Do you allow yourself to think big? When an experience comes your way, do you let it happen? Are you aware of your choices? Have you taken responsibility for your life and how it is working?

Do you make up stories about what is going on? When you meet someone new, do you wait to get to know them or do you quickly size them up? Do fears affect your choices? Do you let others choose for you?

Possibility is such a gift. So many people have clogged themselves with notions based on the past, fears they hold onto, judgments they cling to, and filters that cause them to miss what life actually brings.

Do you miss what life can offer? Have you stuffed yourself with fears, certain ways of viewing things, and past events that taint your experience of what is happening? Are you aware of all the choices available to you? What do you see that limits your life?

So, how can you free yourself? How can you let your experience of the present be unclouded by what has happened in the past? This seems simple enough. The trick is to be completely conscious of all the areas in which you allow the past to influence your perceptions.

If you are conscious, you can decide if you want the past to influence your perceptions. Sometimes this may be valuable, but often it limits your experience.

Taking responsibility for your life and how it is working sets you free. Once you own everything you have created in your life, you can decide to make new choices. You can actually create a new you. At the end of this chapter, we will go through exercises to expose your filters and work on setting you free to live a life you love!

How possibility affects spark:
A free mind allows NEW to happen. It allows you to think bigger, and see possibility. When you see more possibility in the world, do you get passionate, excited, and enthralled with life? When you let a moment happen and stay in a place of curiosity versus feeling that you have seen this before, are you more interested?

The ability to be free is a choice. It requires unlearning routines that don't work for you and silencing your internal critic. The rewards are growing beyond what you already know, getting more within each moment, moving into action, and enthusiastically loving your life.

For example, if you decide theatrical plays are boring because the only play you saw put you to sleep, then how might this affect your desire to see the highly touted new play that has come to town? What if the new play helps you uncover something in your own life that changes how you think? What if the new play evokes emotions in you, opening you up like never before?

Let's imagine you did not enjoy sports as a child, so you are convinced you would not enjoy the company softball team. What if by playing, you find you enjoy the bonding with coworkers? What if you make a new best friend? What if you learn to work better as a team in the workplace and that alters the joy available at work?

From these two examples, we can see that every time we shut ourselves off from something due to past experience, we shut down a new possibility. If you play this out further, you can see that if you allow yourself one attempt at anything to define your feelings, then soon you will run out of things to experience. So how can experience be beneficial versus a curse to Possibility?

All of us have thoughts, beliefs, and ideas from our past. How we choose to utilize that past is where the opportunity exists.

Imagine past experience as preparing you to learn anew in the next moment versus justifying why this moment is going to play out the same way. Is it possible to let your past highlight a new opportunity to practice your life?

Think about children who play on the same swings with the same friends day after day. If they saw that as something they have already done, what might they miss? How do children look at playing on the same swing day after day? What do they get from the experience? How does that differ from how you experience life?

Children have found a way to greet the experience as new. Why do most adults lose this ability? In answering this question, you will find the answer to regaining Possibility and a piece of your spark. Take a moment to write this down in your workbook.

Are we trained that if something sounds or looks familiar, then we should have the answer? Do we choose to be bored with similar experiences versus looking for what is new?

Do children know the value of doing something because of the energy it brings them, regardless of whether they just did it yesterday? Are we trained to try things only once? Do you protect yourself by withdrawing? What is the price of withdrawal?

It is clear that as adults we have learned many things, and often this learning limits our ability to see what is actually possible. Can we learn to free ourselves to see what is possible? Can we remove filters and bring more joy to our life?

What is a filter? An example of a filter is anything that affects how the world comes to us. A filter could be: if something sounds, looks, or feels like what I have experienced before, it must be the same thing. A filter could be: I tried that before and it didn't work, or I asked him before and he didn't want to.

In each moment, how can we see what is possible? How can this time be the time it works? How can this time be the time he is excited to join you?

We each create so many filters, we can't even identify all of them. When you think about all these filters we carry around to prejudge what is happening, it is exhausting. What are we missing? What could happen if we did not prejudge? —Gary Hirsch

This chapter is about freeing your mind to let life and all that is possible happen free of filters, free of fears, and free from past experiences. It is about taking responsibility for the life you have created, so you can see new choices to create a life you love.

How does possibility stay alive?

Gary Hirsch, Co-Founder of On Your Feet: Improvisation for Business

For Gary, **possibility** means to be without fear or judgment of himself or others.

Gary grew up in a home of creation. His family constantly created music, art, and poetry. His 74-year-old mother still takes classes at the local art school twice a week. Gary often woke up to his dad playing Tchaikovsky, and then they would sit down and read the poetry his dad had written the night before. "When we get together, this still happens today!"

It is so amazing to see possibility live, when we are focused on creating things in life. Judgment is a **filter** that kills off possibility by putting focus on what is not possible. Think about this for a minute. Judgment causes us to evaluate what is good and what is bad. When

82

we are thinking about what is good or bad about anything, are we seeing what could be possible? If you instead ask what is possible (absent any judgment), is it irrelevant whether something is good or bad? Does it only matter what is possible and how to create that?

When Gary was young, he remembered being afraid. He was terrified of everything. He was scared of bullies on the playground, severed heads in the closet, and an enormous mouth in the upstairs attic that wanted to swallow him. Even worse, the mouth had a stomach which held a graveyard full of zombies! His dad asked him one night to show him what he was scared of by drawing each monster.

"My dad spent over three hours with me in the middle of the night while I drew these scary beings. He was there the whole time, asking me who they were, what they were named. He said you have made them, so you can control them. If you don't like them, then erase them. It was fantastic. I think it was the first peak into a realization that I was the creator of my own fears."

Gary sees judgment in the same way, recognizing that if he can be conscious of his judgments, then he can see he is the creator of them. They don't actually have to be there, and possibility can live again.

As much as creation keeps possibility alive, judgment and fear kill it off.

"I was really lucky. My parents gave me the front of the refrigerator as my own private gallery, and it was packed with my drawings. I was given an amazing amount of permission to be me. My work was honored, cared for, and inquired about. It was never, ever judged."

In graduate school, Gary was afraid of being an imposter, of being called an expert when inside he felt like a novice. He had to create a showing of his artwork. He didn't know what to do. Gary was paralyzed by self-judgment, asking was this good enough and will people like this?

His father helped him again, having saved all his old drawings in the attic. Gary came up with the idea of a 7/27 show. He would show his 7-year-old drawing and next to it, put his version of the picture at 27 years old. It was a great moment and it was very much Gary.

Self-judgment had killed Gary's ability to see possibility. His father helped him name his fear, and once again possibility became available.

"Judgment is sneaky and stealthy. It doesn't show up all at once. It is super slow. It creeps in incrementally and builds up. Self-judgment squelches the freedom to think, to be, and to risk. If I wonder, will they like me? Will I be funny? Will this work? It kills everything and I am horrible."

Gary has devised a way to catch himself in self-judgment.

"If I start asking, 'should I?' or 'what will they think?', then I know I am already judging, and this kills the possibility to go with what is being presented in the moment."

Gary points out the danger of overplanning and how that kills off possibility. "If you plan something in too much detail, then you often miss the opportunities presented because they don't look like the plan! I think we think and plan a lot because deep down we don't trust ourselves to deal with things in the moment. The beauty of improv is that it shows us not only can we survive, but we can actually thrive in the moment, without any planning whatsoever."

Gary became enthralled with improv (improvisational performance) because of its construct of minimum structure for maximum possibility.

Is life similar? How does structure or fixed ways of thinking/being impact possibility in your life?

He stumbled into an improv performance. There were four performers, and they opened by saying "Hello, we are going to spend the next two hours with you and we don't know what is going to happen." Gary was terrified for them.

84

Gary was spending weeks rehearsing before going in front of an audience because the stakes were so high. "I didn't want to reveal myself to the audience, so I practiced to try and control the outcome."

This improv group didn't have any of that kind of control. During the next several months, Gary spent time rationalizing that he could hardly perform scripted work, so how could he even entertain the idea of improv. His fear kept him away for almost a year. Then, he happened to be listening to a radio program, 'What do YOU Know?' and the interviewer Michael Feldman was an unbelievably natural improviser. "I laughed so hard I almost crashed my car! That radio show drove me to my first improv class. I wanted to feel that way and make others feel that way."

It is important to notice that when Gary saw the possibility (to feel and make others feel that way) he was able to move past his fear.

Gary notices now that he does his best work when he is devoid of judgment and fear. "In order to stop judgment and fear, I have to remember that my past experiences don't really matter, they are here and then they are gone, transient. I can't bottle them, so why try. Tonight is a completely clean slate. If I am relaxed and highly tuned-in to the possibilities around me, then I can be my most creative."

To get an empty brain, Gary first has to realize it is not empty. Then, he decides that whatever was in there is not important now. What is important is happening at this very moment.

Gary comments that he becomes freer with every year. "It is weird, but I have a belief that I will be the most happy when I am older because I anticipate that I will be more forgiving with myself. I will be less inclined to worry about what others think about me, so I can stop playing that exhausting game."

Again, it is important to note that Gary's belief that he will be happier when he is older could limit the possibility that he will be happier now.

What beliefs do you have? How do they limit your possibilities?

Gary realized trying to control everything was keeping him from really experiencing life. "It was paralyzing. It wasn't until improv that I allowed myself to focus on who I was being, the action, what was really happening in the moment, and not the constant chatter of repercussion in my head."

Gary had found his life's work and his passion. The work attracted people he liked into his life. The dynamics of listening and being changed by what he heard affected each aspect of his life. He was able to make a good living. He was exhilarated by the expressive nature of the work, and he was tackling fear each and every time he got up in front of a group.

"I had created my own living refrigerator where I could identify my fears and show myself that it is okay to be me. It was life changing. Each year, I enjoy the journey more and worry less about the outcome. I see so many possibilities."

How do confidence and trust affect possibility?

Kathy Longholland, Serial Entrepreneur

Kathy grew up with a strong sense of self, which she credits to her parents. "I knew I could go for anything I wanted to pursue. That was my foundation. My parents always taught me that I was responsible to make it happen, to make choices along the way, and to live with those choices. They taught me that there will be struggles, but you make it, you keep on keeping on."

Kathy sees many children thrust into adulthood at an early age. "We cut them loose in middle school, saying 'we're done.' My parents were there all the time. They were like the plague; you could not get rid of them. But what they understood was that I was still a child and they were there to assist with decisions."

When Kathy's father died, she fully realized the gift he gave her, "I realized an unconditional confidence in myself as a human being. When he was alive, I always thought it was because of him. But, now

that my rock (my dad) is gone, I see that it is my belief."
Kathy allows herself experimentation. Some decisions turn out good, some marginal, and some not so good.

"You need a really good failure. Failures imprint differently. We remember them. You must move from failure, take the failure, learn, and go forward. Otherwise, you spiral into fear."

If you move through failures and see new possibilities, how is confidence affected? How is your trust affected by seeing that you can handle life?

Kathy's parents felt they taught her how to make good decisions, and that was the best they could do. "They always emphasized a choice, usually when it was poor, by saying, 'That is a choice; how did you feel about the outcome?' I work to instill that message in my kids. They have their choices, their minds, and it is their responsibility to experiment. Sometimes they will fail, but they can learn from those failures."

Kathy feels **possibility** lives when fear is managed or absent. Kathy sees that moving through fear involves trust and confidence in yourself and other people. When you trust yourself, it creates an important base to pursue life.

Kathy started her first of many businesses over twenty years ago. It never occurred to her that she would not survive and be fine. She just had trust in herself. Before then, however, Kathy's last job was a disaster. "I took the job for money, to build a nest egg for my climbing. That was the wrong motivation. I feared not having enough money. I think that is why so many people stay put in their current jobs."

What is so important to notice is that even a disaster didn't derail Kathy from starting her company because she had confidence in herself. Confidence is not tied to being successful. Confidence is available to all at anytime. It requires a trust that we will figure things out, even when we fail.

87

Kathy's mother was also a big influence in her life. "My mom was amazing. No matter what happened, no matter what I did, even if it was big trouble, she would first understand the situation. She would say, 'Let's first get all the facts, and then we can decide what to do. It was liberating, as once you know, then you are free to see what is possible and make a knowledgeable decision."

It is clear Kathy's confidence in herself has created a life where anything is possible.

What would it take for you to develop that confidence? What might be possible for you?

How can possibility live again?

Kasey Mahaffy, Actor

Kasey grew up with very little **possibility** as a child. After his parents divorced, he lived with his dad and his new stepmother.

"It was horrible. Taking care of four boys was not her bag. She just wanted to get her nails done," laughs Kasey.

The only way Kasey's stepmom could cope was to control everything. She quarantined the boys into the family room for the day or outside to the backyard to get her private time.

"She spanked me for having Kool-Aid at a friend's house. I was in bed two hours before my friends during the summer. I could hear them laughing and playing basketball outside my window. Near the end of her rein on us, I had developed facial twitches from all the stress."

In sixth grade, Kasey moved to his mom's house. Life was completely different. "It was sunny skies. I was like a kid in a candy store. When my mom and stepfather were home, they devoted every second to us, and when they weren't, they allowed me to use my discretion. When I first got there, they let me have Teenage Mutant Ninja Cereal and I almost cried. I was so much happier. The facial twitches subsided in two months, and I relaxed into this new freedom.

Maybe too much, as I got a little bit chunky," he said with a chuckle. With this support, Kasey felt loved, respected, and encouraged. Suddenly, life got easier. Possibilities opened up for him. He made friends, had fun, laughed, and enjoyed his childhood.

While Kasey's environment could be credited for his entire shift, that would not be as powerful as noticing that Kasey himself made the shift. Kasey's mom could not force him to see possibility. Kasey noticed that anything was possible after he moved, and this opened doors to fun and friends he had not seen before.

For college, he left town to go to school five hours away. This brought a whole new level of Possibility.

"I was elated. I had the time of my life. I was able to do what I wanted, when I wanted. I made my own decisions, and I was able to be completely free."

During college, Kasey created a four-year relationship. They got engaged, put down a $5,000 deposit on their wedding, but Kasey couldn't go through with it. Through an extremely generous gesture by the girls' parents (they paid for him to see a psychiatrist), Kasey realized he had a significant hurdle (fear) to what was possible for himself.

"I was paranoid that people would not like me. I was so scared that Jessica and her parents wouldn't like me. I knew I was gay, but I cared so much about what others thought. I learned that sacrificing my needs to make others comfortable robbed me of what was possible for my life. I was doing their dance, and I couldn't do it any longer. At twenty-three, I was exhausted trying to please other people."

The counselor helped Kasey understand you limit yourself when you behave the way you think others want you to behave (fear and judgment). He explained that history shows us change has never come out of comfort.

"This proved to be my ultimate freedom. I stopped worrying about others' judgments and if they'd like me. I was born free!"

89

Now Kasey practices his new philosophy, not caring how others will react to his decisions. "I am more of a leader now. My roommate finds my point of view attractive. I'm living by example, which seems to help others. It's contagious."

"Possibility is seeing and understanding all the options available to you at any given time. For me, it meant having to stop worrying about what others think, so I could see those options."

How action creates new possibility?

Mechai Vivavaidya, Founder and Chairman of the Board of Population and Development Association (PDA)

Mechai set out to help his country, Thailand, solve their population problem by reducing the high birth rate in the 1970s and, later, the rise of AIDS. **As he got involved, he realized everyone was talking, but no one was doing anything.**

At this pace, he didn't think things would happen fast enough to make a difference, so he took action. He started handing out condoms and making condoms a part of everything he did, breaking social stigmas along the way.

He implemented the "Cops and Rubbers" program where traffic police gave out condoms and HIV/AIDS advice to motorists. He started restaurants that handed out condoms instead of mints after dinner. He started hotels that had condoms at every corner. He talked about condoms everywhere he went, and he made a difference.

He created an analogy that he was like water, "If I couldn't flow over the obstacle, I tried to flow around it, and if that didn't work, I seeped up from underneath, but I got there."

As Mechai handed out his first condoms, he saw a possibility to hand them out at restaurants. After handing them out at restaurants, he saw that handing them out everywhere made a difference. Without his first action of handing them out, the possibility of handing them out at restaurants, hotels, and other locations would not have occurred to him. Without action, Mechai would not have made such a significant difference in his country!

Mechai also felt that seeing everyone as an equal helped him identify what was **possible**. It helped him see the right action to take. He never saw himself as better than someone or less than someone, more intelligent or less intelligent—no matter his or her position, title, etc. Equality (another potential filter) was a big part of his seeing **possibility**. "We're all just people. Whenever you see someone as below you or above you, then you cannot make reasonable choices with regard to your relationship."

How can you bring possibility alive in your life?
We have discussed how filters, judgment, fear, confidence, trust, and action affect what is possible. Let's talk about each of these areas.

How do you remove filters/judgment? The simple answer is to become aware of having filters or judgment. Then you have access to how that limits the possibilities available to you.

So maybe the more important question is: How can you become aware of your filters/judgments?

How does seeing yourself as better or less than others (equality) limit possibility? How does placing monetary value on things (materialism) limit possibility? How does working a certain way (structured) limit possibility? How does knowing what will happen (past) limit possibility?

Our past experience has created our filters and judgments. Embedding these experiences affects how we perceive what is happening now. Our past can keep us stuck, seeing each experience as a repeat, or it can help us learn to ask new questions, deeper questions, so our current experience is changed.

Some examples:

- A past relationship failure can cause us to anticipate a current relationship failure, or it can provide us new questions to ask so we gain more insight into what is happening dur-

91

ing the new relationship (e.g., why are you pulling away? how do you think we can create the possibility of love in our relationship?)

- One manager would only listen to people when he was finished with the task he had in front of him. He did not like to be interrupted as he had learned it slowed him down. If interrupted, he would at best listen while continuing with his tasks. He noticed that this structure of holding a task above human contact limited his ability to learn and understand people. He saw a possibility to engage when people approached him. He noticed that many of the conversations were insightful and revealed important issues. Until then, he had missed that connection.

Seeking feedback from others is key to seeing beyond your filters. Do you hang around people who think big? How do big thinkers approach life? What limits do they have on how they view the world?

Recall the definition of *innocence*—greeting the moment, unconstrained by the moments that have come before. This takes practice. Force yourself to see the possibilities before considering the barriers or seeing past failures. Picture the possibility in spite of the evidence.

1) Expose your filters and judgments. This may take a few minutes, but try to think through situations where you hold a preconceived notion about something. You may have to notice this throughout the day. Write them down in your workbook as you answer the following questions:

- How does someone's appearance affect your view of him or her?

- What assumptions do you make when you see someone yelling at someone else?

- What do you think about someone who is always happy?

- What do you think when a stranger asks, "Do you have a minute?"

- How do you feel if someone says no to a request of yours?

- How do you respond to your significant other, parent, or child saying, "Hey honey?"

- If your boss asks, "Can I see you for a minute?"
- If a friend or significant other says, "I need to talk to you face-to-face."
- When a child calls your name?
- What other filters/judgments limit your experience?

Think about and notice the times when you filter what is happening. Sometimes these notions or prejudices are accurate, but often they are not. How would things be different if you let life happen as it comes and do not build up filters to the point where you have lived the moment before it occurs? Not only can this be exhausting, it affects how you show up during the real moment.

2) Expose the beliefs behind your feelings. Find something in your life to which you have an emotional reaction. An example might be when someone takes too much time to explain something, so you get frustrated. Write these down. Have you ever tried to move beyond those emotions, saying you're going to just get over this and not have that reaction (e.g., not be frustrated)?

It usually doesn't work, as there is a belief behind the emotion that must change, not the emotion itself. Once you expose the belief, you can examine that belief and decide if it is something you want to hold onto, or see if it is a belief that no longer works for you.

Another example: If you are continually afraid of commitment, saying I am no longer going to be afraid probably will not work in the long term. Take some time to identify what belief is behind the emotion.

In this example, after spending time on it you decide your underlying belief is: Committing will take away my freedom to be my own person. I will have to limit what I want to do.

Now you have a chance to examine this belief to see if it is one you want to hold onto. Is it true? Does committing to someone or something actually limit what you can do?

There may be more beliefs behind that belief. After further study, you decide the reason you think that way is that you think someone better might be out there for you.

93

Again, you can examine that belief and decide if it should hold true for you. Keep working through what beliefs cause these emotions to surface, and either decide to keep the belief as true or change it if it no longer works for you.

What emotional filters limit your possibilities? What beliefs rest behind these emotions? Take a moment to uncover them. How many beliefs are behind your emotions? Keep going until you have uncovered all the thinking that has led to this emotion. Let's get started by writing your answers to the following questions in your workbook:

- If you try something and fail, what does that say about you?
- If someone rejects you, what does that say about you?
- If you are passed over for a promotion, a date, an outing... what does that say about you?
- If someone is angry with you, what does that say about you?
- If someone does not acknowledge you, what does that say about you?
- If you lose, what does that say about you?
- If you win, what does that say about you?
- If you have the best answer or win an argument, what does that say about you?
- If you have the final say or decision, what does that say about you?

After answering these questions, what did you notice? Did you uncover unconscious beliefs that no longer work for you?

Notice when emotions crop up in your day-to-day life. Examine the beliefs behind the emotions. This will allow you to examine the beliefs for validity, and if necessary, free yourself to new possibilities in your life. Sometimes these old beliefs no longer work or never worked in the first place.

What do these filters cause you to miss in life?

How do you move through fear? The simple answer is to notice the fear rising in you and not let it stop you. We often make it mean that if we are afraid, we should stop. While this can be true, most often it only keeps us from what is possible in our life. There really is no magic to this area. It requires noticing the fear, realizing you created that fear, and taking action anyway.

3) Move through one of your fears. Go back to Chapter 1 – Purpose, exercise 2 – Remove All Possible Barriers.

- Select one of the barriers that held you back (e.g., if you were younger, could not fail, would not be rejected, had more money, etc.) and look at what you would do if it were not an issue. Take a significant step towards creating what you would do even though you are not younger, could fail, and don't have more money.

  For example, if only you were younger, you would go back and get a degree. Sign up at a local college for some education counseling to see what it would take to complete your degree.

- (*Advanced*) Go all the way and do it; don't just settle for completing one step. Commit to doing what you would do if that barrier (fear) did not exist and anything was possible.

  How did it feel to move toward something you had previously resisted due to a fear (e.g., being too old, too broke, etc.)? How much resistance to doing this exercise did you notice in yourself? Did you shy away from certain barriers because they would just be too much to tackle? Which barriers were the most difficult to consider? Why? Examine how these barriers limit your possibilities, and write down what you notice in your workbook.

  How can you develop confidence/trust in yourself? The simple answer is to remove the connection between success and confidence. To be confident, it is not required that you first be successful.

As you see yourself continuing to figure things out in life, continuing to make choices and learning, you will develop a trust in yourself that you can handle life.

Confidence is a choice available to you right now. Are you confident you can figure out life as it unfolds? Are you confident you will notice when a choice isn't working and that you will make a new choice?

Sometimes, too much pressure to do everything successfully causes us to stop taking action, and our confidence and trust in ourselves erodes. If you keep taking action and notice some choices work and some don't, but you figure them out, then how is your confidence?

Confidence does not have to be connected to one-hundred-percent effective choices in life.

Let's practice with the following exercise:

4) Make a choice where you are in thinking mode. Take a minute to look at your current situation. Where have you been in thought about something for a while?

- Make a choice to take action. If you notice fear of making the wrong choice, that is absolutely perfect! If you don't have that fear, try to find an area where you are really afraid of making a wrong choice. Choose anyway. Put that choice into action.

  Now that you have taken action, how do you feel? Did your choice work or not? What new choice is available to you?

  Have you associated the success of your choice with your willingness to choose again? Have you learned something from your choice that allows you to choose more effectively next time?

  How can you move to action? The simple answer is to recognize the connection between inaction and planning/thinking/strategizing. Planning/thinking/strategizing actually keeps you from action. The question is not should you plan/think/strategize, but how long do you want it to keep you from action?

Recognize that possibility can only be realized in action. Planning/thinking/strategizing does not create. It may be necessary, but check to see if it keeps you from action (e.g., is it an excuse to not risk failure, to avoid something, and/or to stay in a comfort zone?)

Let's practice with the following exercise:

5) Make another choice following the previous exercise. After seeing if your choice (action) in exercise 4 worked or did not work, what choice is now available? How can you stay in action?

- If your choice did not work, what did you learn? What new choice could you make?

  Make the new choice.

- If your choice worked, what is possible now? What new choice could you make?

  Make the new choice.

How did this new choice work? What did you notice about your ability to discern by making choices and evaluating if they worked? How does this compare to thinking about choices? What is your sense about taking action versus thinking/planning/strategizing?

Powerful grounding questions:
What would my life be like if I was open to "anything is possible?" Where am I limiting myself in this area? What am I blind to? Do I live like anything is possible in life? Are my actions consistent with "everything is possible?"

Signs of excellence:
The biggest sign of Possibility is when you believe you can do anything. People may even call you naïve (take it as a compliment!). What a wonderful thing to be naïve and not limit yourself because of past evidence.

You will see an expansion of people in your life who support bigger thinking. You will notice people propel ideas over the wall versus pulling them back. You will notice ambitious thinkers in your circle.

You will also notice that you see people and their gifts versus noticing their clothes/hairdo/height/weight/etc. This is big!

Another blessing will be when you come across something in life and your first instinct will be to ask questions versus make statements. You will be more inquisitive and less determined to state your opinion.

When you seek what is possible in life, untold oppor-tunities arise.

Chapter 5 - Curiosity

The cure for boredom is curiosity. There is no cure for curiosity.
—Ellen Parr

Definition:
Curiosity is being open and actually seeking the lessons and possibilities life constantly and consistently provides. If learning is one way to enjoy life, then curiosity is the engine for that enjoyment. By keeping curiosity alive, you open up many opportunities to learn.

To be curious doesn't require already knowing the answer. What if the point is to be curious about rather than understanding everything? It requires the ability to continue discovering in areas you have already partially discovered.

Learning is more than taking classes, reading books, and seeking answers on the Internet. To become an expert learner is to open up to the moments in life and notice what is available to you. It requires curiosity.

It is probably fair to say everyone values learning, but does everyone learn in all areas available to them?

This chapter is about encouraging you to become more curious in areas of life that hold lessons. This takes practice and growth. Most of us like to learn and can accept that learning adds joy to our life.

Most of us continue to be curious in the same areas and in the same ways we have always learned. What if you opened up twice the number of areas for curiosity? There are areas you *know* you don't know about, but what about the areas you *don't* know you don't know about?

How do you get curious in areas you *don't* know you don't know about? How would it change your life? Does it excite you? Is it possible? Have you been missing opportunities to expand yourself? What might be available to you in these new areas?

How curiosity affects spark:
Curiosity is so important to spark, as it keeps you going. In many ways, it's what life is about. Curiosity provides intrigue and consistently leads you to areas that throw you for a loop.

Curiosity leads to new opportunities for learning. It is responsible for you coming into a situation wondering what else is available to learn. "If I were to stop learning, I might as well be dead," states Pat Breslin. Learning is the big reason each day holds new possibilities. This sense of newness creates consistent spark and excitement.

Are you still curious? Have you allowed your curiosity to be dampened?

This chapter is about opening your curiosity receptors to pick up more in each moment, not to spend more moments learning. In other words, I advocate becoming incredibly curious in the moments as they occur rather than spending more time pursuing moments in which to be curious.

If you find more to learn in each moment, will you be more intrigued, more aware, and more alive? Will this increase your spark? Will there be more within you to share with the world?

Are you curious about how you can impact the world? How do others respond to you? Each moment, do you notice the ripple you create in the world? Does it work or not work in terms of what you are interested in creating?

At the end of this chapter, we will go through some exercises to open you up to new areas of curiosity and learning.

How curiosity-driven learning can open up your life:

MJ McConnell, Actress and Registered Nurse

As a child, MJ found that her innate curiosity led to learning. The more she learned, the more approval she received from her parents and teachers.

MJ's parents wanted her to have a great life, so they applauded her learning. At the age of fourteen, her mother had been forced to leave school to join her sister scrubbing floors in New York City so they could support the family, and after immigrating to the United States, her father had worked in a sweatshop.

"At the end of a very long shift, my father fell asleep at his sewing machine, and lost a piece of his finger. My parents wanted me to have a better life, and the key to that was getting a good education."

Learning is often encouraged as a means to get something. In MJ's case, it was encouraged in order to get a better life by means of a good job. In this type of learning, it feels like work, something you **have to** do as a way to get something else. Does this remove the joy from the process of learning?

When curiosity drives learning, it comes from a place of fascination, intrigue, and discovery. How is that different? How much of your learning in life is driven by curiosity rather than as a means to get something?

MJ remembers that some of the students in her grammar school were so competitive, getting one hundred percent on tests wasn't enough, so she did extra credit projects to distinguish herself.

"If I got a ninety-nine-percent grade, my mom wanted to know why I didn't get one hundred percent. It was very important that I studied and earned good grades so I would succeed."

After high school, MJ was accepted into the pre-med program at New York University (NYU). Her parents were pleased with her career path at such a prestigious school. However, MJ had had a crisis of the heart. In high school, her true passion had developed—to be a performer.

Her curiosities led her to sing in the church choir and her high school chorus. MJ began acting in the school play as well. This type of learning was magical, since it was driven by her curiosity to explore what she loved.

MJ knew that her parents would not support her studying theater in college because they wanted her education to lead to a respected profession with a secure future. She, too, was torn, because she loved science and as a child had dreamt of becoming a pediatrician.

By the beginning of her sophomore year, MJ came to a startling conclusion: She was not willing to do what was necessary to succeed as a pre-med student.

"Although I went to a college prep high school, I didn't have the Advanced Placement science courses to prepare me to compete academically. I couldn't give up singing in the NYU chorus, performing in the school productions, and spending time with family and friends to devote myself solely to studying."

MJ decided to join her love of science and people with a discipline that would afford her a secure future and the flexibility to pursue performing. She transferred into NYU's Department of Nursing. It was an exciting time, as the nursing profession was developing a body of science and new standards of practice, and NYU's program was leading the way.

At this point, MJ's focus on learning shifted from getting approval to supporting herself. MJ noticed that students were rewarded for being smart, while adults were rewarded for making a living. Again, this type of learning is sought as a way to get something (the label of being smart or the label of being successful).

MJ had never taken music lessons as a child, so she didn't play an instrument. But she was curious about music, and always sang at home with her mother and in church. Her musicianship was self-taught, and with the encouragement of her wonderful high school choral teacher, she was accepted into the prestigious NYU chorus.

"During my freshman year, I sang at Carnegie Hall. It was absolutely thrilling!"

At this point, MJ noticed learning had become part of her passion: to learn for the sheer joy and satisfaction of it. She wanted to become a skilled musician and performer, as well as an excellent nurse.

"There were many talented performing arts students honing their craft when I was at NYU. They went on to win many awards including an Oscar, a Tony, and a Pulitzer Prize. Nursing was becoming an independent and respected profession, and the leaders were at NYU. It was an exciting time to be there."

Is there a difference in spark, when curiosity leads to learning versus learning in order to get something?

MJ graduated, passed her boards, and worked as a neonatal intensive care nurse in the U.S. Army Nurse Corps, rising to the rank of captain. She had many opportunities to perform while in the military. She earned two "Army Tony" awards as best actress and supporting actress.

"I felt very lucky. I could save lives and have the opportunity to enlighten and entertain people through my performing. Serving in the military was a way to thank my country for giving my immigrant father a chance at a better life."

After leaving the military, MJ settled in San Francisco and began to pursue her performing career. She worked professionally for five years, when her curiosity about the craft of acting led her to graduate school.

"I withdrew from making money, auditioning, and amassing additional professional credits to train at a well respected conservatory. It was powerful for me at the age of thirty-one to finally study acting. I was scared, challenged, and happy to realize a dream."

MJ earned her MFA in acting from American Conservatory Theater, and found that knowledge of the world—history, literature, sociology, science, and art— combined with instinct and creativity makes a good actor.

She was now learning in an area that filled her soul. She saw that as she grew as a person, she grew as an artist. As curiosity led to a better understanding of the world and human behavior, she was able to bring more to the table as an artist, and realize more complete characterizations on the stage.

After twenty-two years of working as a professional actor in national tours, Off-Broadway productions, and at many of the most respected regional theaters in the United States, MJ still takes classes in acting, singing, and dance. She continues to learn new skills and plans to open her own theater company.

In partnership with the generous theatrical community, she raises money for various charities.

"Learning allows me to keep up with an ever-changing world and grow as a human being. I am fueled by the desire to make a difference. That's why I am here."

At risk for MJ is if she pursues learning in order to become a great actress, what happens to the magic? If she continues to seek learning out of her natural curiosity, what remains available to her?

At the moment, learning has its own value for MJ. It is not in order to gain approval or make a living; it is enough that it answers her curiosity about what is available in life.

How can you increase your curiosity?
"Where there is resistance in yourself, the greatest opportunity for learning exists. Notice what people cause you to cringe, and what situations repel you; that is where you can learn a great deal, go there," comments Aaron Hornstein.

Once you expand your comfort zone, it never goes back to where it was. As you become used to stretching your comfort zone, you create more and more opportunities to learn by putting yourself in more new situations. Many people see transitions and uncomfortable situations as things to get through, but in these moments rest the opportunity for the greatest learning.

What is in it for you to resist new ideas, concepts? If you emerge from a moment the same as you entered it, have you missed an opportunity? When you resist an idea or someone's feedback, what do you miss out on? Where could your curiosity have taken you? What might have been in it for you to keep discovering?

Another way to increase curiosity is to focus on asking questions rather than providing answers or making statements. If you come from a place of questioning, you will naturally be disposed toward continued curiosity. This is where employing the attitude of being *Chronically Fascinated* shows up.

Friends, coworkers, and family members can provide opportunities to see what you naturally might be blind to, or you might find opportunities through reading, hiring a coach, or attending trainings. For example, you may notice a life lesson repeats itself, but not understand why this situation keeps happening. Others may help you understand how the choices you make, situations you put yourself in, or attitudes you hold cause this event to recur.

Without that insight, it may take you years and several more repeats of the same lesson to learn how you create this situation over and over again. How can you become curious in these areas?

Learning, when combined with action, provides a peculiar and solid enrichment. If, for example, you are interested in art, you will gain much more if you paint as well as look at pictures and read about the history of art. —Eduard Lindeman.

Do you read, ask questions and attend trainings, but fail to take action? How does this show up in your life? When you pick up something new, do you put it into action? Do you try it out? Would that provide a new opportunity for you?

Let's put curiosity and learning into practice by doing the following exercises:

1) Stay in the question. Have you ever noticed people who always have the answer? Have you been that person? Have you entered into an evening or meeting knowing the outcome before you arrive? Have you gone to work already having an idea of how the day is going to turn out?

During the last chapter, we focused on freedom from filters. This chapter, we will focus on curiosity and learning. In this exercise, we will focus on being curious about everything we come across, and we will practice staying "In the Question."

What does that mean? It simply means you have to enter every situation, every meeting, and every conversation asking questions of other people or of yourself. It means resisting jumping to conclusions and solutions. This exercise will help you become more curious about things outside yourself.

- **Get curious about a situation rather than giving advice.** Your friend or coworker comes to you for help. Rather than answer from a place of knowing, you embark on a series of questions to understand the situation and give your friend or coworker your rapt attention. See what you can learn about the situation and about how your friend thinks.

  When you are tempted to reply with the solution to their issues, resist. Instead, continue to ask questions so they can arrive at the answer themselves. This may take the form of: What was your first instinct? How do you think that would affect everyone involved? What was your second choice? What are the pros and cons of that choice?

  Please write your answers in your workbook.

- **Get curious about how someone else sees a situation**. Think of an issue in your life. Instead of solving the issue yourself, ask another person who is not involved in any way to give their take on the issue and describe how they would tackle it. Pick someone who, prior to now, you always thought of as less capable than yourself or lower on the totem pole at work.

(*Advanced*) – Select an issue you are facing and pick someone whose advice you will take (commit to taking their advice and following through with action). Note: You have control of the issue you select and the person whose advice you seek, but to complete this exercise you must take their advice, no matter how uncomfortable it is.

What did you notice? Was the other person creative, helpful? Did their solution cause you to change your final choice in any way? How did it feel to trust someone else so completely? Were you curious during the process? What areas did you find yourself curious about? Were you curious about what you would get from this exercise? What did you learn about yourself? What did you learn about the other person?

Please write your answers in your workbook.

- **Get curious about what someone wants to do.** You are going to see a movie with a friend. Ask what types of movies she most enjoys. Why? Of the movies out now, what most appeals to her, and why? Try to learn more about your friend and what is important to her, given the context of selecting a movie to see.

Notice if you learned more by staying in the question. Did people respond to you differently? How did you like coming from a place of curiosity? Did you enjoy asking questions? Please write your answers in your workbook.

If you can master this technique of staying in the question, not only will you learn more in each situation, you will also be perceived as more valuable by others. You will be seen as someone to help think through issues.

2) Stretch game (advanced). The "stretch" game is challenging and incredibly exhilarating. It expands your comfort zone so fewer things scare you over time. Played correctly, it will free you to take more risks and teach you to face your fears, freeing you from their constricting bindings. Are you curious about what might be in this game for you?

The stretch game allows you to learn about your inner self. You will discover what paralyzes you, what you tend to shy away from, what causes you the most discomfort and why? Be curious about repeat patterns and fears.

To play the stretch game, you will need to find a willing partner. Your "stretch" partner should be fun, enthusiastic, fearless, and someone who follows through. Once you have located a good part-ner, the game is simple.

Give each other positive stretches or dares. These stretches can be done together or separately and reported to one another.

What is a stretch? A good stretch is something that makes you uncomfortable, and the mastery of which will benefit you in the long run. It requires you to do something you initially are scared to do.

How do you become a good stretcher? You take the challenge and do it, and do it immediately. Your reward will be a forever expanded comfort zone. This expansion allows you to experience more in life, enjoy more situations, and, most importantly, learn more about yourself and others. It will open up new areas to explore with your curiosity.

- **Example 1.** It might start out as simple as, "Go talk to that person over there and find out something interesting about them." Many people will find this paralyzing, but with prac-tice, it will become routine and easy. Think of the reward for being unafraid to approach people and talk to them. How often do you avoid doing this? The stretch game can help make it fun to face this fear.

- **Example 2.** It might be to apologize to someone that you have been holding a grudge against for a long time. What could you learn from this stretch? Would this free you?

Other examples.

Go out on a street corner and preach about some topic that is important to you to anyone who will listen. How much of a stretch might this be? Are you curious how others will react to you? Are you curious how you will be in that moment?

Write an opinion to the local newspaper, stating why you agree or disagree with something that is going on. Share your article with several people who generally have strong opinions. Would this expand your comfort zone? What might you learn in the process? How would this benefit your forward momentum?

Engage in conversation with someone or a group of people you normally stay away from, either because you think you won't like them or because you are afraid of them.

Ask someone you have always wanted to meet out for coffee. How might this change your life? What would you be risking? What reward would be there for you regardless of an acceptance or rejection of your request?

It does not matter what the stretch is, only that it challenges your comfort zone, and allows you to see long-term benefit to expanding your comfort zone in that direction. The more resistant you find yourself to a particular stretch, the more likely there is something big to learn by doing it.

After playing the stretch game for a few days, what was your experience? How do you feel now after having accomplished some of your stretches? What was the most difficult stretch? Why? Where did your curiosity take you? What did you learn about yourself in this game? How did it feel to face your fears? Please comment in your workbook.

Powerful grounding questions:
Where is there an opportunity for me that I don't normally see? How could I be more curious right now? Where is there magic waiting to be uncovered? How does my purpose apply here? Where am I stopped?

Signs of excellence:
You will know your curiosity is working for you when teachers miraculously show up in your life. It will be as if you called them to you.

You will no longer see uncomfortable situations as problems, but will see the lessons available to you.

You will stop anticipating life. Instead, you will seek out life in the moment and find learning in everything that comes your way.

You will spend more time living in the question, not going into situations knowing the outcome or answer. You will notice your mind is blank more often, allowing you to discover what is available.

You will see more areas in each moment from which to learn. It will seem as if everything has multiplied, and your senses will be fully utilized.

Creativity is the ability to tap into a wonderful mix of imagination, intuition, and determination.

Chapter 6 - Creativity

I approach a problem like water. If I can't go through it, I figure out how to go around it. If I can't go around it, I try to flow over it, and if I can't flow over it, I look for a way to seep underneath.
—Mechai Viravaidya

Definition:
Creativity is the ability to tap into a wonderful mix of imagination, intuition, and determination. Creativity allows you to move around obstacles, over barriers, and through sticky situations.

Perhaps, the best use of creativity is in creating a unique and beautiful life for yourself. Creativity is much more than the ability to draw or create art or music.

It is the unique blend within you that can solve problems as only you can solve problems. It is the unique makeup within you, which relates to people and draws them out as only you can. It is your ability to create a project with all the elements for learning and joy that only you can create.

You have a special creativity unique to you. As you tap into that creativity, more of you shows up in each moment. This creates more possibilities for magic in your life.

According to Dr. Howard Gardner, there are seven kinds of intelligence where creativity applies:

1. **Verbal** – the ability to communicate effectively and insightfully with others

2. **Logical** – the ability to leverage structured thinking to solve and to share

3. **Spatial** – the ability to create pictures and visually communicate

4. **Musical** – the ability to use music to evoke emotions, communicate, and touch others

5. **Kinesthetic** – the ability to use your body and movement (e.g., sports. dance, or gesture) to communicate and evoke emotions in others

6. **Intrapersonal** – the ability to understand your feelings and to be reflective and philosophical

7. **Interpersonal** – the ability to understand other people and their thoughts and feelings.

Each of these areas offers opportunity to apply your own creative abilities. You may find your talents are more pronounced in some areas. Are there areas you have never explored?

If you draw from each of these areas of creativity, what can open up for you? How will this add to your ability to connect with people and experience life?

What are your special creative gifts? What do others notice about you? How can you bring your creativity into new areas of your life? How will this enrich your life? How can your creativity enrich others lives?

How creativity affects spark:
Creativity is important to spark because it is an application of your unique ability to make a difference.

The more you tap your creative side to solve problems, communicate, or show up for people, the greater your opportunity to affect life in a powerful way.

Have you used your creativity to solve a difficult problem? How does tapping into your creativity affect your spark? If you could use your creative talent on any occasion, would it bring new options to life? Would it give you new excitement and energy?

Creativity can open paths of communication that go beyond words. For example, a college graduate really wanted a job with the top advertising agency. He was competing with hundreds of applicants, so he worried about how he could stand out. He decided to Fed-Ex a full-size door to the hiring partner with a note that simply said, "I'm going to keep knocking on your door until you hire me." He received an offer letter the following week!

How do you think his use of creativity added to his life in that moment?

Life offers so much fun. How can you take advantage of the creative opportunities constantly available to you? Are you missing them? How can you notice each opportunity, have fun with it, and make a difference?

How creativity brings new possibilities to life:

Scott Newman, Innovator and Inventor

Scott Newman grew up on a small farm where he became self-sufficient. It was a necessity to be effective in all areas since others weren't around to help. Scott learned to be creative in solving his problems. He notices an opportunity when there is a gap between what is and what could be.

"I constantly share my ideas because it keeps the process moving forward. Even if the idea starts out sounding ridiculous, I keep going. I like to search beyond the obvious, especially when someone says 'it can't be done.' That drives me."

Scott believes creativity and innovation happen when there is time. He recognizes we are so busy, living from appointment to appointment, that we rob ourselves of time to be creative.

"I need moments with nothing to do, to just sit and think. I have never liked having a full schedule. My friend's father always told him to keep some extra money saved, just in case something really great came along. I do that with my time. I keep extra time, just in case I need to be especially creative."

Do you take time to see other solutions available in your life? Where is your life stopped? How can you utilize your creativity to bring that part of your life alive again? What is possible?

Scott learned in ninth grade football that it is easier to run around the big guys than to run through them. He notices the same thing in life. We usually try to go through things instead of taking time to find a creative way around them.

What obstacles are in your life? If you take time to tap your imagination and intuition, is there a creative path?

By spending time with Scott, it becomes obvious his creativity goes beyond solving problems in his life. He uses his creativity to bring joy into his life.

"I have this amazing group that gets together to swim each day. We talk about life and help each other see bigger possibilities for ourselves. I love to use my creativity to highlight new choices in my friends' lives." Scott surrounds himself with friends because it makes life fun. They laugh with him along the journey, add to his creativity, and help him find new answers.

"I am always amazed at who helps me. Sometimes the most creative advice comes from people I didn't see as creative. In the last five years, I have sought help more than I ever did in the previous years combined. Now, I get through things faster. Last week, my wife asked 'is it plugged in?' and she was right. It helps to involve others early. I know I would have kept looking for something much more complex."

How could you involve others in your life to enhance your creativity? What might they see that eludes you?

Scott has developed a personal board of directors to help him navigate life. It is another example of how Scott's creativity brings new possibilities into his world.

How creativity leads to action:

Tammy Gilley, Artist

Tammy grew up with busy hands. She was always doing something, from sewing doll clothes to making Indian jewelry. "I got my creative streak from my mom. She has always exposed me to all kinds of ways to express myself."

Tammy usually goes through different creative phases, from art to writing to verbal expression.

"It depends on the outlet I need. Sometimes I just need to purge. Lately, I have gotten tired of hearing what I have to say, so I have turned my energy toward art," laughs Tammy.

It is hard to imagine being creative and not moving to action. In Tammy's case, she is her best self when she is in the act of creating. "Creating fuels my spark! I am out making a difference with people."

As a child, Tammy had a flair for drama. In her seventh-grade English class, she chose to write a play, "Millionaire in Distress!" Tammy acted out all the parts.

"It was a murder mystery. I thought I was the next Norman Mailer. The class actually thought it was fabulous! I remember I got applause from the kids, an 'A' from the teacher, and a request to continue with the upper-level writing course."

Tammy's desire to share was driven by creating the play. It is important to notice that creativity's outlet happens in action. How can your creativity call you into action? How would it enrich your life?

Tammy's mother encouraged her to try new things. "I never was intimidated, and I always felt free to try anything. My mom loved everything we did. Her reaction was always great; it immediately went onto the fridge. There was never a wrong approach. I grew up without judging what I did."

Her mom instilled fearlessness in Tammy to try anything. Tammy was always into new projects, seeing what she could create. As she became older, a loud inner critic developed. It started during high school when she began to worry about what other people thought.

"I wasn't as innocent and free as when I was a kid. That tainted the process, and I focused on the result of how it looked, which killed my creativity. I stopped doing a lot of what I loved."

How does looking good affect your creativity? What takes you out of action? What stops you from creating a life you love?

As an adult, Tammy realized looking good as a marketing representative had again caused her to stop being creative. Her focus was on the results of her sales efforts. "I stopped writing. I stopped spending time in my studio doing my art. I was missing myself."

Tammy credits journaling with turning herself around. "Journaling keeps me centered and on top of the noise. It helps me notice when I get stopped."

Tammy has learned to let go of others' reactions to her work, positive or negative.

"Creating is an opportunity for me to be with myself for better or worse. I don't hold back; whatever comes out, comes out. It's not about making, it's about expressing, and I constantly change those expressions. I am at my best when I just see what happens."

Tammy again finds her creativity leading her to action, which causes her life to take on a renewed sense that anything is possible.

"I hope to define and create my dream job. I know it will center on working with people, possibly coaching creativity. One thing is certain: It will be a whole new creative process for me, and I'm looking forward to it with glee!"

How you can be more creative:

A recent study found that children five years and younger are able to generate ninety percent original ideas amongst each other. By age seven, only twenty percent of the ideas are original. As adults, only two percent of the ideas are original.

How is creativity lost? Are we too self-critical? Do we limit what is possible? Are we afraid of being laughed at? Do we stop exploring? How can you train yourself to see possibilities where you used to see barriers? How can you use your creative genius to figure things out versus being resigned to why it cannot be done?

Gary Hirsch describes an exercise, "When I am stuck or blocked, I play a game. The game is nonsensical. I see an object and describe it completely different than I normally would. For example, I see a door and I say it's permeable, it's soft, it flies, it goes nowhere, etc. I find this opens up new possibilities for me. It is part of the training I learned in studying improv techniques."

The idea Gary describes trains you to see other possibilities even if they don't make sense. Try to make it a habit to stretch your problem-solving skills to come up with more and more options for everything. This makes the world a bigger place, and opens up new doors for you.

If you feel stuck and depleted of ideas, another exercise is to write out on paper everything that is in your head. Exhaust your mind, and make sure it all gets down on paper. This opens up room for more to develop and new creative ideas to emerge.

Is your creativity affected by the people in your life? Does your group inspire you?

The energy of a group of possibility *seers* is unbelievable. It is hard to be glum around people who only see how something *can* work.

Lastly, consider nature. There is something special about nature, which frees the mind to think of new possibilities and see things previously unclear to us. Nature could be the park down the street or the end of a drive up to the mountains.

Let's do some exercises to increase creativity:

1) Explore the seven areas of creativity within you – Are there areas of your creativity you have yet to tap into? Have you practiced bringing your most creative self to different situations? Let's look at each of the seven areas and understand how you might tap into them.

> • **Verbal** – the ability to communicate effectively and insightfully with others. What are your greatest skills in talking with and listening to people? Take a minute to write down your thoughts.
>
>> ° What are ways to be creative with how you talk and write to others?
>>
>> ° Under what circumstances have you had to be creative with your approach to speaking or writing?
>>
>> ° Do you use your best, most creative verbal skills at work?
>>
>> ° In your personal life?
>>
>> ° When arguing?
>>
>> ° When you are frustrated?
>>
>> ° In a group setting? Do you modify your approach in a group?
>>
>> ° With children?
>>
>> ° Where do you most often forget to be creative when speaking or writing?

Now write down what you notice from the answers above. What insights do you find in reviewing your verbal creativity?

> • **Logical** – the ability to thoughtfully leverage your logic to solve and share. What are your strengths in reasoning through a situation? Take a minute to write down your thoughts.

° What are ways you can be creative with reasoning through situations with others?

° On what occasions have you had to be creative in using your logic?

° Do you use creative logic to find multiple solutions to problems?

° At work? In your personal life? Is it different?

° To unlock or tap into your emotions?

° To love people as they would like to be loved?

° To find supportive and nurturing friends?

° To uncover areas where you can put your natural abilities to best use?

Now write down what you notice and what stands out to you from your answers above. What insights do you have in tapping into your creative logic?

• **Spatial** – the ability to create pictures and visually communicate. What are your creative strengths in using visual communication? Take a minute to write down your thoughts.

° What are ways you can be creative visually?

° When have you had to be creative with drawings or pictures?

° Can you visually communicate things that are difficult to talk about?

° Is your visual creativity reserved for art? Where else could you employ it?

° Is this area suitable for work? For expanding relationships? How?

Now write down what you notice from your answers above. What insights do you find about your visual creativity?

- *Musical* – the ability to use music to evoke emotions, communicate and touch others. How are you creative in your use of music or sound? Take a minute to write down your thoughts.

  ° What are ways to be creative with how you use music and sound with others?

  ° Under what circumstances have you had to be creative with music?

  ° Are you creative with music during meetings, gatherings, dinners, presentations, or proposals?

  ° Do you ever make your own music? Or play an instrument?

  ° Do you write music or songs?

  ° How do you employ music to set your mood? Does it soothe you, rile you up, or get you going?

  ° In what untried areas might it be interesting to utilize music?

  ° How does music affect you?

Now write down what you notice from the answers above. What insights do you have regarding your musical creativity?

- *Kinesthetic* – the ability to use your body and movement (e.g., physical body, sports, or dance) to communicate and evoke emotion in others. What are your greatest skills in utilizing your physical self to communicate or express yourself? Take a minute to write down your thoughts.

  °What are ways to be creative with your physical self?

  ° Under what circumstances have you had to be creative by using your body and movement?

  ° Where is your best creative use of your body and movement?

  ° When do you notice your body being an asset?

° How does your facial expression affect your communication?

° Where do you not notice how your body is communi-
cating?

° Where do you limit your creativity regarding movement and your body?

Now write down what you notice from the answers above. What
insights do you have regarding physical creativity?

- **Intrapersonal** – the ability to understand your feelings
  and be reflective and philosophical. What are your greatest
  skills in leveraging how you feel? Take a minute to write
  down your thoughts.

  ° What are ways to be creative with your feelings and
  thoughts?

  ° Under what circumstances have you had to be creative in sharing your feelings?

  ° How can you be more creative in understanding
  yourself?

  ° Do you develop your own philosophies about life?

  ° When are you reflective?

  ° How can you be more reflective in moments of frustration, anger, or fear?

  ° Do you usually share your feelings?

  ° How can your feelings guide you?

Now write down what you notice from the answers above. What
insights do you have regarding your intrapersonal creativity?

- **Interpersonal** – the ability to understand other people
  and their thoughts and feelings. What are your greatest skills
  in understanding others? Take a minute to write down your
  thoughts.

    ° What are ways to be creative with how you listen to others?

    ° Under what circumstances have you had to be creative with your approach to understanding others?

    ° Do you use your best, most creative listening skills at work?

    ° In your personal life?

    ° When arguing?

    ° When you are frustrated?

    ° Do you modify your approach in a group?

    ° With children?

    ° Where do you most often forget to be creative when trying to understand others?

    ° What is your ability to connect with and listen to others?

Now write down what you notice from the answers above. What insights do you have about your ability to listen to and connect with other people?

2) The fishermans game (by On Your Feet) – the idea is to go far away from yourself (e.g., think like a fisherman) to get back to yourself in a deeper way. Think of a situation you are facing at work or home.

Now, list all actions a fisherman would take if facing the same situation in their world. It is important to list actions, not intentions.

For example, if the problem is that your colleague undermines your initiatives, a fisherman facing another fisherman who undermines his attempts to catch fish, would:

- Move to another part of the ocean

- Cut the other fisherman's nets

- Haul his fish in faster

- Develop tamper-resistant nets

- Catch other types of fish, join forces with the competing fisherman

- Sit down and ask the competing fisherman why he is ruining his haul

- Ram the other fisherman's boat

- Hire an interfering boat to occupy/distract the competitive fisher

- Go out to fish at an odd time of day where he couldn't be found

- Get a boat that could go where the other fisherman could not go

- Let the other fisherman think he was ruining his catch while secretly hauling in all the fish

Next, write down what that action is about. For example, hauling in his fish faster is about improving his technique. Developing tamper-resistant nets is about designing a solution that can't be sabotaged.

Next, analyze what the action is about and apply that to your situation. How could you improve your technique or design a solution that could not be sabotaged? As you play the fisherman game, you should come up with several different creative solutions to your situation.

In playing the fisherman game, what did you notice about your own creativity? Did you come up with something that worked? Did you feel you were creative in playing the game? Was it easy for you to become the fisherman? How can a game like this help you with other situations you face?

Powerful grounding questions:
What would a fisherman do? What other possibilities exist? How can I be incredibly creative right now? What limits am I imposing?

Signs of excellence:
First and foremost, your life will be open to any possibility. This will bring incredible excitement to how you live life.

You will notice the avenues you could choose, each with its own set of possibilities and opportunities.

Other people will seek you out for "out of the box" thinking and brainstorming on issues.

You will automatically see multiple solutions to situations you are facing and be able to help others expand their possibilities.

You will feel like you have many options to create and express yourself. You will find yourself evaluating the seven areas of creativity and how they apply in different situations.

Your life will interest you.

If you have discipline to create your life, you take actions consistent with your purpose. You choose your attitude in each moment. You notice how choices affect your life. Discipline enables you to notice your feelings and still take action.

Chapter 7 - Discipline

Don't ask yourself what the world needs; ask yourself what makes you come alive. And then go and do that. Because what the world needs is people who have come alive. —Harold Whitman

Definition:
Discipline calls you into action and allows you to be fully alive! Discipline is the difference between wanting a life you love and creating a life you love.

Discipline is about action and choosing in the moment. Where is your opportunity to take action? Where do you procrastinate? What takes you out of action? What would make a difference in your life?

If you have discipline to create your life, you take actions consistent with your purpose. You choose your attitude in each moment. You notice how choices affect your life. Discipline enables you to notice your feelings and still take action.

For example, Jesse was afraid of public speaking. This fear held him back in life. One of Jesse's Purposeful Endeavors was being the campaign manager for a politician. Public speaking was critical for him to accomplish his job. Jesse always found less powerful ways to perform his job and avoid public speaking. This left Jesse with less spark because he was not being the person he was committed to being.

What would it take for Jesse to notice his fear of public speaking and still take action? How would it change his power to create a life he really loves? How might this fear show up elsewhere in Jesse's life?

Another aspect of discipline is creating a process to get back to who you want to be when you are not living as your Purposeful Self.

People with spark develop daily practices to get back to their Purposeful Self: spirituality, silence, retreat, and play are a few. These practices involve reconnecting with what you are committed to creating.

How discipline affects spark:
In connection with taking action in spite of fear, discipline is critical to living a life you love. We all are afraid in life, but developing the discipline to take action in the face of fear will open new possibilities for your life.

If you can notice that a **reaction to fear** is causing you to procrastinate, you can develop the discipline to take action in spite of the fear.

When you have the discipline to stay true to your calling in life, you create a life that fills you with passion, energy, and enthusiasm. You may also have a practice that returns you to your best self when you have lost focus on what matters in your life.

Discipline involves focusing on what you are committed to and not managing what you have no chance of controlling. This eliminates worry and anxiety, which waste energy. Worry and anxiety do not create; they are thinking exercises and do not live in action.

Worrying is like paying interest on a debt you may never owe. —E. Dave Mendenhall.

It is critical to keep your energy high, since it allows your natural creativity and passion to emerge. How do you utilize spirituality, playing, silence, nature, or other practices to replenish your energy? Do you notice when you are not being your Purposeful Self? What discipline have you developed to return to being the person you are committed to being?

How the discipline of replenishment creates spark:

Tricia Brennan, Minister

Tricia grew up in a large family. Her family was Catholic, and she was exposed to extensive religious theology. Some theology was puzzling, some great, some negative, but Tricia sorted through it.

"I was so spiritual as a child. I had a real personal relationship with God. I lived a prayer life, always talking to God. I had such a sense of power in myself."

Tricia's connection through spirituality gave her tremendous confidence that she could make a difference in the world. As life moved on, Tricia became more fearful, worrying about what other people would think and how they would react. She yearned for the simplicity she felt as a child when she had no question about her purpose.

Now Tricia is disciplined in noticing when she strays from her Purposeful Self. What came so naturally early on has become more complicated. Tricia sees the world as more mucky, political, and lacking protection. Somehow, fear crept in.

Tricia misses her boldness.

Tricia journals, meditates, talks to God, or reads Gospel to get back to her best self. She feels each practice leads her back to who she wants to be. For example, Tricia began as a social worker by helping the homeless. She opened a shelter that housed many families. Everyone was under enormous stress, as each family was squeezed into a single room.

"I noticed that when you are poor, you have to fight more and be strategic. To be effective, it is not all pretty and easy. You can't avoid the hard work. It is part of moving justice ahead."

Tricia was afraid things would go wrong. She did not want to make a mistake and feel foolish or have people get angry. Tricia found prayer and meditation. "It's not that prayer melts all the fear away. Prayer allows me to see something much bigger than myself—a source of love. The more I love, the more my fear becomes secondary."

Tricia began organizing groups to take the fight where it needed to be taken. It was an "in your face" approach, and it demanded a great deal. "I was a wreck for the first six months. Prayer kept me from feeling alone; it kept me connected with humanity. It broke me out of my own little world, so I didn't feel sorry for myself."

Some of the parents in the shelter impressed Tricia with their ability to maintain some sense of normalcy for their kids. She remembers them helping with homework even though they were living in a car or the close quarters of the shelter.

"These families handled so much and under such duress. They inspired me with their loving commitment to their children." For Tricia, praying cleared the clutter. She was able to hear the still, silent voice of God calling, and it was life giving.

"Powerful prayer lets me be two capable hands and one big heart in the world. I am inspired to be loving. While I fail in that every day, the impulse is there, and I trust it. Being loving gets me out of the fail/succeed mentality."

Tricia decided to stop practicing as a Catholic, not agreeing with the role women were given in the Church. She enrolled in Divinity School to become a minister. "Now, people talk to me all the time about their faith, and I cannot think of anything more important for me to do. I enjoy being a part of those conversations."

Tricia is enjoying her growth as a minister. She feels people bring her closer to God. "It's not that I don't get disappointed or have conflicts with people. I do. But, I live within the ideal of grace. I am grateful for what I do have. I have a sense of abundance. I see my life as ordinary, but I have been able to find what is extraordinary in my ordinary life."

How the discipline to choose confidence creates spark:

Frank Fredregill, Striving for Balance

Frank is committed to living a great life. He accomplishes this by being his own best friend. At first, this seemed difficult to grasp, but as Frank explained, it seemed like magic.

"I can be in any group and any situation and coach myself through. You can put me anywhere in this world and I am with my best friend. I am very giving to myself. It's not that I don't need other people, I absolutely do, but I have confidence that I can figure life out."

Two events provide examples of how Frank creates an amazing confidence by showing up as his best friend. After college graduation, Frank undertook a solo bike ride from one United States coast to the other. His trip took four and a half months. He went through seven tires and logged between twenty-six and one hundred eighteen miles per day. One day, it was so windy he had to pedal while riding downhill or he would have come to a dead stop. He ended up riding seven thousand miles alone.

"Who else do you turn to? As my best friend, I had to have the discipline to do what was right, to know what I wanted, to push myself, and to encourage myself. It was freeing. I knew I could do it. I need other people to see new aspects of myself and to awaken me to new things, but I can affirm my value in this world."

On his bike trek, Frank recognized that he lacked control over many things, particularly Mother Nature—he was almost hit by lightening. Frank chose his attitude and his will. His confidence made his journey an amazing trek across the country. After what he was able to do in one day, Frank decided not to take any day for granted.

Another event that stands out was the time Frank decided to swim from Catalina Island to the mainland in 1985. He was just the fifty-seventh person to complete the swim. Now, nearly twenty years later, only one hundred people have accomplished this difficult task. Frank coached himself through the swim. He had to soothe his fears about being a shark's meal. Again, it took discipline to stay with it.

Through his different experiences, Frank has developed a discipline to notice the clues God sends his way. He contemplates their meaning and follows what is right for him. One of the best clues he received came from the side of a school wall he was driving past. It said, "It is easier to build children, than to rebuild adults." Frank has confidence in his ability to be a great father to his two daughters. Frank sees the amount of spark discipline brings to his life.

"There are two voices in my head, one that is generally the loudest, and one that speaks to what would be courageous. The courageous voice is usually quiet and promotes the path of greatest personal challenge. So many people want comfort in their life. What is wrong with discomfort? I think we miss opportunities if we don't have the discipline to face discomfort."

Frank sees people are uncomfortable being challenged on whether they know what they want in life. He believes one secret to happiness is being clear on what you want.

"So many people don't go through the process to understand what they really want. And I think that is a big mistake. There is a saying that says if you don't know what you want, then you won't know when you have it. And since having what you want makes you happy, not knowing means you'll never know if you're happy."

Frank decided what he really wanted in life was to hold his wife's hand as they walk the beach and be proud of the job they did as parents. He also wants to be the oldest person to swim the English Channel, at seventy years of age.

"I told that to a life insurance salesman and he didn't like my answer. He needed what I wanted to cost more money, so he could show me how much insurance to buy. But, I am comfortable charting my own course."

Frank's philosophy of being his best friend has provided him with an incredible peace, which few seem to get. His father's license plate, which was about achieving peace, reads - 'A few do.'

How the discipline to separate from your random thoughts creates new possibilities:

Heidi Henzel, Marketing Consultant

Heidi had a protected, idealized childhood. From the beginning, she knew who she was and had clear intentions and spiritual connectedness.

"I was sensitive to what was happening around me. I chose to be clear from the outset. I could understand the motives and intentions of others, which gave me confidence because I could more easily assess situations and outcomes."

Heidi used her discipline to experiment with separating from her daily thoughts. In seventh grade, Heidi began to explore how she could think about nothing.

"My mind was active, like everyone else's—life, the many 'to do's,' current news, world events, routines, and daily activities. I began to wonder, what would it be like to be fully aware without thinking? I was curious to understand my mind and patterns of thought. It became a form of meditation."

Heidi remembers when she first cleared her mind of everything. "It was liberating. I was so quiet and peaceful. I was able to relate to others without distractions. I was completely present for someone else. It freed me to explore what was possible."

Heidi found that this ability drew other people to her. They sought out her perspective. "In high school, many friends would seek advice about their relationships and problems they faced. It was natural and common for this to happen. I would listen and offer alternative ways to look at things. I had my own set of questions I was pursuing, free of the typical teen insecurities."

Heidi developed a discipline to move beyond her internal dialogue to create what was possible.

"I really think it is simple. Each of us has an amazing power to create our lives. I think we have to get clear about what choices we are going to make, then make them, and notice what that creates. Then, we can evaluate and choose again."

How you can create discipline:
If you can imagine a life you love, discipline is the key to actually creating it. Discipline will help you move beyond contemplating, thinking, analyzing, considering, weighing, and dreaming to actually being who you want to be.

How can you be powerful in making choices? How can you move into action where you currently are ignoring, putting off, and denying? How would your life change?

Let's try a few exercises to develop discipline.

1) Discipline over your mind – Release worries. What is your mind running with right now? Write it down. Is there anything you are worrying about? Add these to your list.

Can you do anything about the items on your list? If so, commit to an action and cross them out. With the remaining items you cannot do anything about, imagine placing them into a bubble one at a time.

Once you have placed all the items in the bubble, add your worrying mind and close the bubble. Picture pushing the bubble out into space with a string tied to it. This will allow you to retrieve it at any moment and reclaim your worries should you want them back.

But for now, release them into space and imagine your mind clear and uncluttered. Focus on your mind being blank and still. Keep going with this exercise until you have the bubble a long ways away and your mind completely blank. If need be, retrieve the bubble and keep adding things if your mind comes up with new worries, including worrying about not worrying.

How does it feel to have a blank mind? Do you feel refreshed? How do you think you can keep your mind blank? What do you notice? Please write your answers in your workbook.

2) Create a discipline to center yourself. Take thirty minutes and go to a retreat, preferably somewhere with nature (e.g., a park, the hills, a tree outside). Take nothing with you except a pad and pencil or pen.

Remove all distractions. Concentrate on being absolutely still and silent for the first ten minutes. After you have been still and silent for ten minutes, connect to a power greater than yourself, whether that be your God, nature, the universe, Buddha—whatever works for you, but connect to that power.

You can connect to your power source by prayer, by bringing that source into focus, or by simply being still. Feel the strength of that power. Imagine yourself refilling and becoming your most amazing self, your Purposeful Self.

Stay in this process for the remaining time. Know you can tap into this power at any time by being silent and connecting.

How was this experience? Was it easy to connect to your power source? Was it easy for you to become your Purposeful Self? Do you have a picture of who you are as your most amazing self?

If not, spend some time writing in your workbook. Who would you be if you were your most amazing self? (Refer to your Purposeful Self statement).

How is your energy level affected as you become your most amazing self? Please write your answers in your workbook.

3) Create a discipline to let go – Play. Do you still take time to play? Have you ever been someone who played regularly? Do you have children in your life?

Children can be great teachers and playmates. For this exercise, simply find an activity that would be considered play, preferably something requiring physical movement (e.g., a game of tag, hide-and-seek, red light/green light, leapfrog).

Try to pick a game having little or no competitiveness to it, as this exercise should involve laughter and leave you feeling light. If you don't have playmates readily available, play a game by yourself (e.g., hopping up and down on the floor in your office and picturing everyone asking what you are doing). Again, creating a game that evokes laughter may provide the best renewal. Now simply play the game for a few minutes.

How did playing feel? Was it easy for you to play? Did you laugh? Were you able to find playmates? Was it comfortable for you to ask others to play? Please write down your answers in your workbook. Do you have a replenishment routine? If not, how would you create one? How often would you replenish? What would you do?

4) Create a discipline to take action. Do you notice choices that are still waiting on you? Can you be afraid and still choose anyway? Will you learn more by choosing or by thinking about it?

Imagine you are like most adults and have *choice constipation*. Your job is to clear out all the unmade choices. Please answer the following questions:

- What are you currently worried about?
- What occupies your thoughts?
- Which people do you have conflicts with?
- What are you putting off?
- What things are people asking you for that you are still thinking about?

Please write your answers in your workbook. Now, go through the entire list and pick the first action that comes to mind for each item.

What stops you from taking that action? What happens if you take action? What happens if you don't take action?

Who are you being right now? Is it consistent with your Purposeful Self?

Which choice moves you in a direction of creating a life you love?

All that is left is to take action on that choice. Take the pressure off yourself by noticing that most choices in life can be cleaned up if they don't create what you intend.

How did it feel to imagine choosing in all these areas? How would your life move if you made all these choices? What are you committed to creating?

Please write your answers in your workbook.

Powerful grounding questions:
What choice is in front of me right now? What actions could I take right now? Can I choose even though I am afraid of the consequences? What choice creates a life I would love? What am I committed to? Who am I committed to being?

Signs of excellence:
You will know you have discipline when your plate is continually clear. You will make choices as they arise.

You will feel confident you can create a life you love in any circumstance. You will quickly notice areas of your life where you are avoiding, ignoring, and denying, and then take action on those areas.

You will have discipline to keep your energy at a high level. You will notice when you are out of balance and immediately enter your process to center yourself.

You will notice that single events do not completely absorb your thought process. You are able to maintain a sense of perspective, as seemingly bad situations do not overwhelm you. Instead, you are able to see them within the bigger picture of life.

Your environment is what supports you or distracts you, so being intentional about creating a support- ive environment is life altering.

Chapter 8 - Environment

If your environment is a reflection of where you are in life, and your life is affected by your environment, which do you change first? —Tamra Fleming, Life Architect Coach

Definition:
Environment is the world you create around yourself. It includes your home space, office space, hangouts, movie/TV/book selections, other media selections, and what surroundings you put yourself in. Your environment is what supports you or distracts you, so being intentional about creating a supportive environment is life altering.

There is a separate chapter dedicated entirely to the people you choose to include in your environment.

How does your home affect you? How does what you read propel you into your Purposeful Calling? How do your hangouts support you in being your Purposeful Self?

How environment affects spark:
If you create an environment that makes it easy to live your life on purpose, you have set yourself up for success.

Do you choose easy?

Many people believe if life is hard, getting there is more rewarding. Is it more satisfying or just harder?

If you choose easy, will you have more energy for other areas in your life? How does choosing easy play into the environment you create for yourself?

143

Let's say your purpose in life is to feed the world. You have a choice to listen to the nightly news, which highlights stories of starvation and despair, pointing out disasters from around the world.

Or, you have a choice to read the Red Cross newsletter, which highlights how the efforts of thousands of people fed four hundred thousand people in Africa last month.

Is it harder to stay excited about your mission if you watch the news? Does it propel you on if you read the Red Cross newsletter? Does it affect your energy level in either case?

Do you pay attention to the environment you create for yourself? How does your environment affect you? Which parts of your environment make it easy for you to stay fresh and enthusiastic? Which areas distract you?

Choose environmental factors that inspire you to live your purpose and be who you want to be. Be conscious of your home and what is in it. Does it refresh you? Does it cause you to get excited about creating your life? Do the colors, possessions, and artwork calm you, or do they agitate you?

Do you have clutter? How does clutter affect you? What does clutter represent? How does discipline come into play when clutter is present?

When you go to outside activities, parties, or movies, do these propel you forward or dishearten you? Notice the choices of what you let in, and how those choices affect your attitude, purpose, and energy level.

How environment choices affect energy:

Tamra Fleming, Life Architect

Tamra is an absolute sparkplug! She radiates excitement and enthusiasm. Her purpose is helping people create the life they want. Her mission is to assist people to operate on their "highest vibration" level!

144

Whatever Tamra does to sustain her energy level is worth copying, as she is vibrating at an amazing level.

In Tamra's business, she interviews clients about their life vision and helps them create an action plan to achieve it. She then tours her clients' homes and businesses to see how their environment reflects what they say they want.

"Everything in life is constructed of energy, and everything outside in your physical world is a reflection of your thoughts and intentions."

To support her clients' vision, Tamra reviews color selections, areas where clutter is present, and functional use of the space to create clarity in the environment. She notices what is out of alignment and then asks her clients what they would like to do about it.

For example, one client was looking to attract a relationship, yet her bed was only big enough for one. Another client wanted to be clear and focused in business, but his office was clogged with old papers and old business, distracting from new business.

Where is your environment out of alignment with your life? What area of your life is not working? How does your environment affect that area?

Tamra has clients rate everything in their home on a zero to ten scale, with ten being the highest vibration and zero being something that is draining their energy. She recommends people consider eliminating anything below a seven.

"I feel like I have always had a natural eye for balance and beauty. I like my space to tell a story of who I am. Several years back, I designed my foyer to recreate the experience of walking onto a 1920s train station platform, complete with period luggage, fog machine, and train whistle. It was thematic and added fun to arriving at my home!"

Tamra also pays attention to clutter.

"Clutter equals unconsciousness. The more conscious you become, the better you can see what is not in alignment in your life. Clutter is

145

a great place to start. I ask questions that bring focus to the real issues. Our belongings hold memories and energy. I like to focus on what energy the 'things' are representing in people's lives."

Tamra believes it is critical for people to create an environment that supports being conscious, especially in our fast-paced culture.

"We are bombarded in our society by messages of how we *should* be. Only by remaining completely clear can we either eliminate these messages from our environment or recognize that we don't buy into them."

Tamra notices that she starts to lose balance in her life and environment when she gets tired. Being tired is a warning sign that she needs to become more conscious in the moment. The process of reordering and clearing clutter helps her regain her energy.

What takes you out of living a life you love? How do you make a practice of noticing?

Tamra sets an amazing example of how paying attention to your environment can dramatically affect your energy level.

How can you create an environment that supports you?
The biggest thing you can do to improve how your environment supports your spark is to notice.

Notice how your physical space makes you feel. Is it cluttered? Is it comfortable? Does it support you? When you are in it, do you feel energized?

Notice how the media you select or allow in affects your energy. Does it get you going? Does it depress you? Does it inspire you?

All the interviewees spent significant time sitting with nature to get away and refresh. In the last chapter, we mentioned nature in terms of replenishment. How can you build replenishing components into your environment? It was uncanny how almost everyone spoke of how spending time in nature had an impact on his or her spark! It was interesting to notice.

Do the books, television, movies, and magazines you read support your spark? Do they inspire you? Do they leave you worried or fearful?

Let's focus on a few exercises:

1) Unclutter – Set up your home to make certain it supports your energy level and brings you peace and harmony.

> • **Clean up** – clear all stacks and piles. Clean out old mail, sort through old magazines, recycle, put laundry away, and clear your home of clutter.
>
> How did this feel? Was your home messy? Did the messes drain your energy every time you walked by, saw them, and thought about cleaning them? Can you keep your home free of clutter? How will that serve you? Please write your answers in your workbook.
>
> • **Clean out** - using Tamra's scale of zero (it means absolutely nothing to you) to ten (the item completely speaks to you), go through your home and rank every item as you walk through. Remove, sell, or give away any item that is a six or below.
>
> How did this feel? Were you able to rank many items at or below six? Were you able to get rid of them? Are you attached to material things?

Did you notice what characteristics the items that were seven and higher held? Did they have anything in common? Please write down your answers in your workbook.

2) Re-choose your inputs – It is important to select media that supports your purpose and enhances your energy level. List all the TV shows, books, magazines, radio, newspaper sections, and types of movies you read/watch. As you are listing them, rank on the same scale, zero (does not support my energy level) to ten (inspires me to go for my purpose), with a five being neutral. Remove or stop anything that is four and below.

How does your media support you? Did many on your list propel you forward? Did any drain you?

What other inputs might be good for you to add? Please write your answers in your workbook.

Powerful grounding questions:
Does this give me energy or is it draining? What could I add to my environment that would light me up? What inspires me about my space? Where is there an opportunity to clean up clutter?

Signs of excellence:
You feel more centered when you wake up and start your day. It is easy for you to get started on any of your Purposeful Endeavors.

Your reading materials, home, and radio programs enhance your energy level. You love being inside your space (home, office, car, etc.).

You notice that people in your life, the groups you are involved in, and the media you allow into your environment all propel you forward.

Taking great care of your physical body by paying attention to exercise, food, and rest, enables you to perform as your best self.

Chapter 9 - Health

The doctor of the future will give no medicine, but instead will interest his patients in the care of the human frame, in diet, and in the cause and prevention of disease. —Thomas Edison

Definition:
Good health requires an awareness that your body plays an important part in living your life to its fullest. Taking great care of your physical body by paying attention to exercise, food, and rest, enables you to perform as your best self.

Good health involves making the connection between the treatment of your body and how your body is able to support your life.

Does your energy level affect your attitude? Is it difficult to perform as your best self if you are run-down? Do you connect exercise, food, and rest to how you feel?

How health affects spark:
Good physical health is a core need. In the hierarchy of needs, it must be taken care of before you can put your energy into your purpose.

How is your physical health? Does your physical condition take energy away from what you want to accomplish with your life? Where do you succeed in supporting your best physical self? Where do you fail? Exercise? Food? Rest? How would your life be different if you excelled in these areas?

Which is most difficult for you to maintain?

The first area of focus, and the easiest to comprehend, is sleep and rest. Sleep is a natural period within every twenty-four hours when the body repairs itself, tests its systems, consolidates memory, purges itself of cellular waste, and stockpiles energy for the day ahead. On average, humans spend one-third of their life asleep! Adult sleep needs range between five and ten hours per night, with the average being seven to eight hours per night.

Did you know that too little sleep can make you sick? A University of California at San Diego study showed some immune-system activities decrease as much as thirty percent after nights where over three hours of sleep are missed. According to a 1993 U.S. National Commission on Sleep Disorders and Research, thirty-six percent of us don't get enough sleep.

What gets in the way of a good night's sleep? Conversely, how does a poor night's sleep get in the way of your life?

The second area of focus, with many theories on the best plan to support your best physical self, is food. How important is food to your energy level and well-being? Are you consciously aware of how food affects your body?

In general, as mass food production increases, food contains more preservatives and fewer vitamins and minerals than in the past. To counteract this, it is important to be more conscious than ever about what you put in your body. There are many competing thoughts on the best way to eat. However, it is generally accepted that fresh food is better for you than preserved food.

Regardless of the nutrition information you subscribe to, it is important to become aware of how food makes you feel. I noticed that foods heavy in refined sugar exhausted me, prompting me to cut doughnuts, cakes, cookies and other highly sweet items out of my diet. The joy of eating these foods was not worth the low energy I experienced.

Do you connect food with your energy level? Do you connect your ability to fully live your purpose with your energy level?

The final area of focus is exercise. For many people, exercising regularly is a struggle, a constant battle. However, many other people develop exercise routines that are a fantastic part of their day, and they have no trouble exercising.

How does exercise fit into your life? If it is difficult, what makes it difficult for you? Does lack of exercise keep you from achieving your goals in life? If it is difficult, does it have to be? How might exercise be easy for you? How does exercise affect your energy level?

Nothing great was ever achieved without enthusiasm. —Ralph Waldo Emerson.

On this journey, make your commitment to physical fitness a life-long one. Sometimes, it is not the number of hours you put in, but how often you put in those hours that creates a healthy balance.

Positive perseverance will lead to good results in this area. Perseverance is not a forced path. It is a patient path that continually unfolds in your favor.

Are you patient with your exercise routine? Are you patient with your food and rest habits? Do you allow good health to continually unfold in your favor?

Physical fitness is never ending; it begins anew each day. Choose to enjoy the journey, as there is no destination.

In this chapter, you will have the opportunity to review your practices and see if they support you.

How to create a positive health routine in your life:

Darcy Winslow, Nike Global General Manager, Women's Footwear

Physical health has been a core part of Darcy's life since she was five years old, the age at which she joined the "Surf Club" swim team.

"I remember there was a diving pool that was twenty feet deep, and I just ran and dove off without warning. I landed flat on my stomach doing a huge belly flop and ended up with a bloody nose. I bounced up, blood dripping from my nose, into my mouth, and down my chin, and shouted, 'This is great!'"

Okay, so you may not respond as enthusiastically to a bloody nose as Darcy did, but don't miss the joy that physical exercise can bring to your life. As Darcy playfully states, "Exercise is like drinking orange juice; you're doing something really good for yourself." As children, exercise is considered playing, and it is fun! As adults, exercise becomes something that has to be done.

How can you make exercise "playing" again? How can it be one of the best parts of your day?

"I find when I get a workout in each morning, then no matter what happens, even if the day goes to hell, I've already done something good for myself. And no one can take that away. It just starts the day on a good note."

Darcy found she could test life out via physical challenges, sports, etc. Moving from player to coach, she was able to be a leader, a planner, and a facilitator to test her abilities in those areas. Moving from gymnast to cheerleader, she was able to put herself on the public stage, and allow others to criticize her. Through these "tests," she learned how she felt about herself and began to understand how others saw her. She was given a chance to be comfortable with that level of scrutiny. Darcy was able to get much more from exercise than a workout.

Can you create exercise to coincide with other areas of your life? Is it possible to look at exercise as a tool in your life to figure things out?

By pursuing physical activities, Darcy found she learned a lot about what she was capable of doing.

"I always challenge the 'can't' to understand 'why can't I?' How *can* I? What will it take?"

This natural curiosity about what is possible has moved into other aspects of Darcy's life.

"In sports, I am constantly in a position to confront obstacles. I take risks. This practice has given me more confidence in other areas of my life. It is so much easier to explore new professional fields and take on new roles."

Darcy has held two mantras in life:

1) Try a new sport each year—forty-seven to date! (This keeps exercise fun).

2) Stay in good enough shape to avoid having to turn down an opportunity (e.g., a challenging mountain climbing expedition). This keeps the possibility open.

She has succeeded in never turning down an exciting experience, no matter how physical.

"Staying in shape allows me to experience the world so much more, and leaves so many doors open. When I travel, the first thing I do when I land is go for a run and see the city by foot. I see it so differently than when traveling by car. I never know what I am going to see. It is so personal. I remember my first run in every city."

On one run, she was with a friend in a remote city in China, where Americans are rarely seen. Two locals were riding their bikes, entranced, watching the runners. They were so entranced that they continued toward each other, oblivious, and boom, they completely took each other out.

"Interesting and unusual things happen all the time when you get out on foot and see a city. You never know what is going to happen!"

How can staying healthy fold into your strategy for living a life you love? How has Darcy connected staying healthy with her purpose in life?

Darcy feels maintaining her physical self is a discipline in personal responsibility. "There is so much ahead of me, at least as much as there is behind me. I want to be at the top of my game so I don't read about things. Anyone can do that. I want the experiences. Someday I want to go to Tibet and make it to base camp!"

Whatever Darcy decides to tackle, her success will not be a surprise. She competed in her first triathlon before she owned a bike, and came in fourth!

How does the practice of discipline allow Darcy to continue to enjoy exercise? How does the chapter on discipline apply to physical health?

Today, Darcy has taken on yoga as a new focus, and she cannot wait to jump out of bed each morning.

How to get a positive health routine back into your life:

Lindsay Andreotti, Partner and Founder, Brilliance Enterprises

Lindsay has noticed three significant physical stages thus far in her life:
- Childhood - when she developed confidence through sports
- Career/husband/kids - when she abandoned her physical focus
- Realization – when she connected her health with who she wants to be in the world.

As a child, Lindsay was always physically active, dancing and play-ing/running in the woods. As she moved into sports, she became a strong soccer player. It was her sport, and she excelled. One day the track coach saw her play and commented, "With your speed, I'd love to see you in track."

Lindsay wasn't interested because she didn't know track, and she was already great in soccer. However, the track coach wanted her on the team, so he kept after her. One day at lunch, he orchestrated hav-ing the five cutest track guys recruit Lindsay. He figured this to be his best chance, and he was right. Lindsay quickly agreed to try out for track.

The coached pushed her further by suggesting hurdles. Lindsay was afraid she would never get it. She struggled and kept falling. In her first race, she did a complete face plant. Lindsay would cry, get angry, and want to give up, but the coach kept after her. Lindsay eventually made it to the State Championships in hurdles.

"It taught me how to believe in myself, and I had the hardest time with that. Now, it translates to what it takes to get over hurdles in the non-physical world. I have to believe in myself."

Track turned out to be an incredible experience. Lindsay went on to win as the anchor leg on the 400-meter relay team in the league championships. She beat women in the final leg that she had never outrun before. She ran the race of her life. To this day, it stands out as one of the greatest experiences of Lindsay's life.

"I learned I was blinded by being comfortable (soccer), and I cut off other opportunities (track). The experience has forever changed me. Now I let my curiosity lead me, and I am open to new stretches. It was a great life lesson."

Where are you cutting off opportunities? How could you risk comfort to gain more for your health? Do you have someone to support you in staying committed?

Lindsay acknowledges that in her physical life, guides have been the key to getting beyond the mental story she tells herself about what is possible. In addition to her high school coach, her husband helped her reconnect to her physical health. "My husband believed in me and supported me until I believed in myself. I know if I was left to my own devices, I probably would have given up. To this day, I don't like the treadmill. But I love nature walks and hikes. It's fun now."

Last year, Lindsay hired a personal trainer. Lindsay sees how her physical routine opens her creative abilities. She feels brighter and more aware. "It's not about losing weight. Being really physical lets out the trash. Then there is room for great stuff to come into my life."

Lindsay believes we are beings of mind, body, and spirit. She had ignored her body for fifteen years. "Being balanced in all three (mind, body, and spirit) is so important. We are challenged to grow

in all three, and they are so intertwined that I get motivation in one
for the other two. Forgetting my body was stupid. It was so limiting,
and I am excited to be back."

As for eating, Lindsay admits she still occasionally makes bad choices, so she has to work out more often. "I have made the connection
between what I put into my system, and how that affects me, so now
I have less work to do in the gym. Once in awhile I mess up, but it is
moments now instead of months."

Lindsay sees herself continuing to try new hurdles in life and
remaining committed to her physical self. "I need this body to last
long enough for my spirit to do its work!"

How can you take care of your health?
It is a simple recipe to take care of yourself, and there is little mystery in this area. However, most people struggle. Exercise, good
food, and rest are simple ingredients, so why is there struggle?

The key is connecting the feelings of being in top physical condition
with the actions needed to create it. What we discussed in the chapter on discipline is very relevant here.

Let's focus on some exercises to embed good health practices in your
life:
1) Exercise – Daily. The most difficult area seems to be daily exercise.

"I needed someone to get me going for the first several weeks until I
became hooked on how I felt. Then, I didn't want that feeling to
change, so I kept at it. My husband kept me going until I could
choose it for myself. Without him, I don't know if I would have made
it part of my daily routine," said Lindsay Andreotti.

Until you make the connection with how great you feel, whatever you
need to keep yourself going is the key. Another key is to make it easy
and fun (make it feel like it did when you were a kid). Start out doing
something you really enjoy. Tie it in with something else you really
enjoy. For example, if you love talking to a certain friend over coffee

each week, change the routine to talking during a morning walk. Pick a time that cannot be easily filled with other things. Early mornings may be best, as it is unlikely you will have things come up. Set yourself up for success so you can stick to your routine.

"I exercise first thing in the morning; that way nothing can get in my way. Even if I have an early morning, I can get up earlier that day and keep to my routine. It makes me feel great for the rest of the day, so I don't want to skip it," states Jim Terney.

Don't hesitate to get help. Hire a coach. This doesn't have to cost money. Find a disciplined friend who will agree to be your coach. Call them at the same time each morning to report how your workout went. Walk through whatever issues you are having, what is getting in your way, and what you are telling yourself that keeps you from what you want to have.

This support is crucial to set new patterns and break through barriers. "I had tried to include exercise in my life several times. I was unsuccessful at making it an ongoing part of my life, so I asked for help this time. I hired a friend and we talk once a week about my goals, where I'm getting stuck, my failures...and now after twelve weeks, I feel I am on my way. I don't need as much support," states Joe Zaniker.

- **Start out** - Perform some form of exercise for seven straight days. Do not critique it or worry about how strenuous the exercise is, just do it everyday for seven days.

  Notice how you feel. Please write in your journal what was easy and what was hard about these seven days. Can you take away what makes it hard? How can you make it easy? What did you enjoy about the process?

- **Routine** - Create a routine that is easy to stay with. Don't worry about making it long or strenuous, just do something every day. As it becomes habit, you can increase the length or difficulty of your routine. Initially, however, just make it easy and fun.

What did you notice? How routine is your routine? Is it fun? What would make it easier?

- **(Advanced)** Establish goals that can be reached in two to four weeks. Set times and distances you want to run or walk within. Set weights you want to be able to lift, etc. Create one or more goals you can achieve.

  How did it feel to reach your goal(s)? Was it easy? What was the key to your success?

2) Food awareness - Once exercise routines are in place, it is natural to start noticing how different foods make you feel and at what times you should eat. There are many conflicting theories on food and diet, so I won't advocate one over another, but I do suggest noticing which foods and regimens best support your physical body. Connect the way foods make you feel and start eliminating foods that reduce your energy level. Leverage the discipline you learned in exercise to focus your eating efforts.

- **Awareness** - Identify foods that decrease your energy level. Write these down. Identify foods that support your best energy level. Write these down.

  What did you notice? How many foods do you consume that decrease your energy?

- **New food** - Find new foods that support your best energy. Read books or research on the Internet, but keep adding to your list. Educate yourself about food.

  What did you notice? How does food play into your energy? How does food play into staying healthy?

- **Discipline** - Create a discipline in yourself that has you eating fewer and fewer energy-reducing foods. Pay close attention to food and how it affects your best physical self.

  What did you notice? How did you change your eating habits? Was it easy? Are certain foods more addicting?

3) Good rest habits - Let's create some practices around rest and sleeping. Do you have issues with sleeping? Do you regularly sacrifice your ideal sleep time?

- **Sleep amount** - Identify your ideal sleep needs. As discussed, most adults need five to ten hours of sleep per night, with the average needing seven to eight hours. So, let's start with seven and a half hours of sleep per night for one week.

  Keep a journal each day to notice how rested you feel. Noting that exercise and food will affect your energy level, sleep has been intentionally saved for last so you can isolate its affect once you have created a good exercise and food program.

  After one week, did seven and a half hours feel like your ideal sleep time? What did you notice? Could you perform at your best with less? Do you need more?

  If needed, adjust your sleep time and stick with it until you identify your ideal sleep time.

- **Interruptions** - Now that you understand your ideal sleep requirements, notice what else interrupts your best night's sleep.

  Are you stressed? When is your last meal? Does your mind race? Do you take any medications? Is there anything that gets in the way of your night's rest?

  Begin to isolate the issues and create a game plan to eliminate them. If your mind races, create a strategy where you write down everything on your mind so you can pick it up in the morning and let it go for the night.

  If you are stressed, create a relaxation routine by having a warm cup of decaffeinated tea, taking a warm bath, writing out your thoughts in a journal, meditating, or doing whatever causes you to release your stress.

If medications are bothering you, check with your doctor to see if you can take them in the morning. No matter what gets in your way, continue to isolate it and work to eliminate it.

What did you notice? What was getting in the way of a good night's rest? How were you able to eliminate it? Please write your answers in your workbook.

Powerful grounding questions:
How does this support my health? What is my commitment to my health? If I lived like my health really mattered, what decision would I make right now?

Signs of excellence:
You will know you have made it, when staying physically fit is no longer a struggle—it's an enjoyable part of your routine. It has become a healthy addiction. You will notice that you feel great, and that you crave feeling great!

You will start to notice an incredible connection between food and performing at your best. This will give you a discipline you never held before. You will be able to say no to foods, not because they do not tempt you anymore, but because you elevate the cost of how you will feel over the satisfaction of eating the food.

Your outlook each day will be that you can tackle anything. Your energy level will remain high throughout the entire day.

When relationships work in your life, they bring you to your Purposeful Self. Your relationships reflect your performance in creating a life you love.

Chapter 10 - Relationships

A great relationship is best served when one's love for each other exceeds one's need for each other." —Dalai Lama

Definition:
Relationships are people you actively develop and maintain connections with in your life. This group can support you in living your purpose or they can move you away from it.

One of the most important factors in our lives is who we choose to surround ourselves with. These people are a mirror. They represent where we are and what we think about ourselves. What type of people do you surround yourself with? What do you look for in your relationships? Who do you select for friends?

If your relationships really work, they should call you into being your Purposeful Self. Your relationships should align with creating a life you love.

How do people show up in your life? How do you show up in their life?

When you are aware of how you show up for other people, you can test it against your Purposeful Self. You can learn which relationships take you away from your Purposeful Self. When you are conscious of how other people show up in your life, you can also test who you are being that would cause them to show up that way.

Do you choose the people you spend time with? Do they choose you?

When you are choosing people into your life, you look at how they affect you. If you rely on others choosing you into their life, you may miss needed people in your support structure.

What qualities are important to you in selecting people? Do you have people in your life who are inconsistent with those qualities? How might your life be different if everyone in your life propelled you towards your best self?

If you take a moment to survey your relationships, you might notice how they serve as an indicator about your life. Relationships show where your life is currently heading, what you are creating in your life, and who you are being in the world.

How do the people in your life describe what your life is about?

The great thing about the mirror other people are to you is how it gives you choices. Now you can decide if you like the choices you are making, or if you want to create new choices.

Have you created relationships that assist you in being your best self?

If you look at yourself as the person responsible for creating your relationships, you have the ability to create new relationships with the same people or with different people.

As discussed in Chapter 2, you are always at choice. How active are you in creating the relationships that fit into a life you love?

How relationships affect spark:
People play a huge role in supporting you to live your purpose in all three areas (Self, Calling, and Endeavors). Relationships affect how big a game you play in life by how they call you to account for what you say you are committed to.

Relationships allow you to share and learn during your journey. How do rich, rewarding relationships affect your enjoyment of life?

Look at the people you have chosen. How are they a reflection of where you are in life? Are you ready to play a bigger game? What kind of mirror do they hold for you? Do they show up in life just like you do? Is this a welcome realization or a wake-up call?

If you can get clear on your purpose, the people you choose will be able to grow with you and enjoy the journey. Otherwise, you may find that as you grow and evolve, you have to move on from people either because they don't want to go where you are going now, or because they view life in a way that no longer works for you.

I know that if I don't lose touch with some of the people who are trying to reach me, I'll lose touch with myself.
—Martha Beck, Life Coach

People are the biggest factor in your environment, so it is crucial for you to choose people who support your Purposeful Self. How do the people in your life affect your spark? Which people enhance your energy level? Which people drain your energy? What purpose do the energy-draining people serve? What roles do different people play in your life?

People can help you stay conscious by alerting you to choices made and their outcomes, or they can prevent you from becoming conscious by shifting your attention from what makes a difference in your life.

In this chapter, we will focus on relationships and how they can propel you into living a beautiful life.

How others create relationships that support their life:

Linda Devers, Healer, Artist

People are Linda's passion in life, and that is where she focuses her energy.

"Whenever I get off my path, it is because I am focused on making money versus how I can show up for people. If I stay focused on people, life works out beautifully."

167

Linda recalls she had a strong sense of who she wanted to be as a child. She stayed true to who she wanted to be even when it meant she might not be liked.

"In fourth grade, I was told to let a boy win in a chess match because boys don't like to lose. I realized I didn't either, so I beat him. I wasn't going to cave in and not be myself for someone else's comfort. I don't think that serves anyone, especially not me."

Do you sacrifice yourself for relationships? Are you true to who you want to be in the face of disagreement?

Linda continued to follow her passion of connecting with people and bringing them together. Linda has developed her own group of friends that she calls a tribe.

"In nature, if an animal gets cut from the herd, they usually die. I think it is similar with people. Outcasts in our world really struggle."

Have you created a strong group that supports you being your Purposeful Self? Who are the key members of your tribe?

Linda's tribe is patient and caring. "We can be vulnerable and show up as who we are without judgment. There is acceptance and forgiveness. This allows for greater risk taking, so I can learn at a much faster pace. As I go through major transitions in my life, I need support. This is such an amazing group of people in how they encourage me to take action in my life. We hold space for each other to be bigger."

Do you create relationships that call you to be bigger and more full?

Linda notices that many times other people see more in her than she sees in herself. "People have really helped me see who I can be. Once I found my calling in life, I was comfortable being in front and leading because I knew this was what I was meant to do. I would not have gotten there without the encouragement and help of my friends."

Linda has enjoyed great success personally and professionally from the relationships she has created. She has also had lots of laughter along the way.

"My friend Nancy and I have been friends for more than forty years. She is the reason I went to college! Pam and Sandy have been friends for decades. We have opened businesses and traveled the world together."

Linda's partner, Liebe, helped her see that she must draw. "She looked at drawings I did in high school and just stopped in her tracks and said "You MUST draw." Once I started, I couldn't stop. Without her, I would not have figured out how my Purposeful Calling could encompass all of me."

Linda's Purposeful Calling is to use her energy and creativity to heal and bring joy to the world.

How do relationships help you determine what you want to create in your life? How do they help you remain true to what you are committed to?

Linda continues to foster connections with people. She is always finding new people to bring into her tribe. "I bring mutually beneficial people into my life. It doesn't have to be equal, just mutual. I don't get caught up in keeping score. That can make you crazy, and it is the wrong place to focus—it's much better to focus on learning, growing, loving, and supporting each other."

Are your relationships mutually beneficial? Are they loving?

Linda has compassion for people, but she enters relationships knowing she cannot change people nor do their work for them. "I am more discerning of which people I spend time with now. I have always believed in people, but sometimes I carried them along. Today, I spend time with people who are committed to being amazing. It's so easy to see what's amazing in people when I look, and now more than ever I find that in people. And what's magical is when I hold a space for amazing people in my life—I begin to see the amazing qualities in everyone."

How others have moved from fitting in to powerfully choosing their relationships:

Joe Zaniker, Passionate Artist and Owner, Graphic Focus

Joe grew up on a remote wheat farm near Wasco, Oregon. It was a small farming community, and there weren't many people around. "My sister and I loved people watching. We never went camping because we wanted to go places where there were lots of people."

Joe remembers how he wanted to fit in. In watching footage of his second birthday, he was amazed to see that he gave his gifts away. "I loved the joy of how everyone responded to me. I learned to give so I would get back. As I got older, I had a tendency to buy things for people so they would like me."

Do you have your own version of fitting in? How does it affect the relationships you create?

Joe remembers how when he entered school, he believed there were two kinds of people—those who were safe to be around, and those who were not.

"I learned to change myself based on who I was with in order to survive. I worked on blending in and not standing out. I was great at avoiding certain people in school. I remember in third grade, one kid in P.E. was running laps and someone picked up dog poop and threw it on him. I knew I wanted to stay away from him because he was a target and I didn't want to become one."

In high school, Joe developed greater skills at fitting in.

"I had become capable of manipulating people, and I could join just about any group. I could hang out with the stoners or the jocks and be okay. My motive wasn't to be with them or to be popular, it was to be safe."

Joe ran for student body president his junior year and won. He was selected king of every dance except one.

"The reason was I didn't stand out with any group, so it worked to my advantage in terms of getting by. Now, authenticity is what I strive for, but back then, it was about surviving. It was interesting because I deeply wanted to belong, but I knew my future was not going to be with these people."

Joe sees many people walking through life as he did in high school. "So many people are just surviving. They don't have a handle on who they are and what they stake their life on. They don't see they are generous, loyal, kind, focused, enthusiastic, etc. That is why the movie 'The Matrix' was so brilliant. People thought they were really living, but they were actually asleep."

What is the cost of surviving? Do you survive in your relationships? Or do you create amazing relationships that leave you feeling unstoppable?

It was not until his twenty-year reunion this past summer that Joe realized how he had showed up in school.

"I really missed my classmates, and I understood how connected we had been. I am gay and I knew they knew, but I didn't know how they would feel. I didn't care because I was comfortable with myself, but it was amazing to be welcomed with open arms by everyone. I was really interested in them, so they were interested in me. We had a lot of fun together. I didn't expect it."

After the reunion, Joe looked at his yearbook from high school and read what people had written. "I thought I was just getting by the whole time, but now reading what people said, I see it all so differently. I was the one everyone came to when they had a problem. Everyone seemed to say, 'you were always there for me.' I was surprised; I had not read my annual since I graduated."

Do you show up for people in ways you don't even realize? Have you asked people why they are in a relationship with you?

Today, Joe is deliberate in choosing relationships. He knows he has to judge people to see who he wants to spend time with, but he wants to be with people and not be judgmental. This is easier when he focuses on being his Purposeful Self.

"As I mature, I see the difference between making someone 'wrong' versus deciding this is someone I choose not to be around. I'm not perfect, but I am enjoying the practice."

How are you in relationships? Do you choose who you want in your life?

Joe sees how all people affect his spark and at the same time, how no one affects his spark. "People can do things to evoke my love, joy, sadness, etc., but no one can take those from me. I need people to have spark, but spark is my choice."

Are you able to sustain your spark around others? How can you generate who you want to be when you are afraid you won't be accepted?

"Fear is a great initial motivator, but I don't think it is sustaining. Fear works in advertising, but not in living a wonderful life. I work hard to be who I really am as that sustains my spark. I am funny, spiritual, kind, loyal, generous, creative, and empowering. But, I have been deceitful, manipulative, and mean-spirited as well. When I am truly who I am, the people in my life behave with me as they truly are. That is when the right relationships develop in my life."

How others have found the magic available in relationships:

Rick Durden, Professional Pilot, Aviation Attorney, and Author

As a boy, Rick grew up learning a great deal from his aunt. She was a single parent who taught at schools around the world, and she had a profound effect on his view of people.

"She taught me a great deal. I loved her insights. When I was six years old, there was a big bully in the neighborhood. She told me to look at him, even if I didn't like him, and find something I could learn from him, to find something interesting about him."

Rick initially rejected the thought but later became friends with the big kid, finding out he was an only child who was lonely and seeking attention. They played basketball together, with the big kid eventually helping Rick to make the varsity team.

Do you miss what is possible with people you meet? When you see beyond the surface, what is possible?

As early as he can remember, Rick wanted to fly. In eighth grade, Rick joined Boy Scouts when a friend showed him how it tied into a flying club. Rick was able to take his first flying lessons at a reduced cost.

Rick's aunt later got him a job at the local airport. She emphasized the value of education and said he need not worry about school; she would make sure he had enough money.

"I was able to reach most of my goals in life because of other people."

Do you miss opportunities people bring into your life? What opportunities do you create for yourself and others inside your relationships?

Rick was motivated early on by two things—curiosity and fear of missing something. His aunt was instrumental in this, encouraging him to look around each corner, to go to a foreign country and eat where the Americans don't, to learn from others— especially outside the United States—and to learn from people throughout history.

One of Rick's barriers was shyness. He saw others as smarter and a lot cooler than himself. He assumed others would not be interested in him.

"It takes a while for the teenage years to die off, and to grow up past that."

What ways of being hold you back in your relationships? How could you be courageous and create relationships you would love?

Now, one of Rick's great joys in life is meeting new people. He seeks out people he can learn from. Twice a year, Rick and a group of pilots fly vintage airplanes to a location where they create their own adventure.

In winter, they use skis to land on frozen lakes and in summer they switch to floats. "We just show up, and over the years it has become one of the most enjoyable things in my life. With these people, I sometimes laugh so hard I wonder if I'll be able to stop."

What magical groups of people have you created in your life? Where are there opportunities to create such groups?

Rick knows there are many interesting people out there, so he decides who he wants to spend time with. He doesn't want to be around people just for the sake of being around people. He seeks meaning in his relationships, and avoids large groups, figuring the collective IQ of a group is ten points lower than the lowest IQ in the group.

"I learn from most people. I find I learn most effectively from people I like, because I am relaxed and comfortable. If I have negative feelings about someone, I tend to be aware of the negatives and therefore not as receptive to learning. However, if I can get past those emotions, I sometimes learn more from those I initially dislike."

Where are there opportunities for you to go beyond what you initially dislike in someone? What is there for you to learn? What relationship is possible as a result?

Rick has invested considerable time and passion developing his ability to select friends.

"They add so much to my life. We share the great times and the bad times. We assist one another with invaluable advice, and we face tough issues together. The thought of losing that group of people would be devastating to me."

To build those friendships, Rick felt the most important thing was to listen. "I don't learn when my mouth is open. I also notice that I am considered a good conversationalist when I don't say much."

The second most important thing is to empathize. "I try to see what the other person is going through and understand who they are. If I am listening, I am more likely to see that."

How relationships bring learning to life:

Aaron Hornstein, Healer

Aaron immediately makes his presence felt as he enters a room. He is a big force. Aaron starts by talking about spontaneity and how it brings newness to life.

"I have given up certainty. It is an illusion. I just let life happen; it is so much easier."

Aaron believes people are the biggest cause of both spontaneity and uncertainty.

"When I meet people, I change. I never know what is going to happen or how we will relate, but I am forever different. Who knows...if I meet one thousand more people, I might be a completely new person. My thinking keeps getting bigger and bigger."

What do people bring to your life? Who do you learn from?

Aaron learns from people in two ways, by understanding something he never knew or something he thought he knew, but with a new twist to see it more clearly. He recently adopted a new strategy to learn from those he wanted to avoid.

He began by asking why he was avoiding these people. Aaron realized he was seeing in them what he didn't like about himself. He recalled a woman who laughed way too much for the situation and how it made him angry. It was the people-pleasing aspect that upset him. He was angry for selling out his feelings to please others.

Do you avoid certain people? What could be available to you by choosing these people?

Aaron began putting himself into situations with people he normally would avoid. Each time, he learned so much about himself that he became fascinated with the process.

One night, while walking home from a meeting at 10 p.m., Aaron noticed three homeless teenagers across the street. His first impulse was to speed up and pass them without making eye contact. But in keeping with his new motto, he crossed the street and began talking to the teenagers.

As had been his experience, it turned into an amazing evening. He stayed until 4 a.m., spending six hours out on the streets talking about the kids' lives. Their outlook on life inspired Aaron.

What inspiration awaits you in unknown relationships? How might you create more opportunities?

Aaron started out believing in himself. "I was born not needing anything. I had a great family. I had a great body and mind. I was intelligent and talented. But, somewhere my thinking turned on me. I thought I had to have hardship to feel real."

Eventually, Aaron found his hardship—AIDS. He knew when he found out that he had a choice to be angry and hate, or find forgiveness. Intuitively, Aaron realized if he chose anger, he would die.

Today, Aaron sees AIDS as a gift. He learned love, surrender, how to live in the present, and how to appreciate life. Aaron also learned to open up to people he never would have talked to before.

"The lessons I have learned are far greater than the pain I have suffered. I don't fear death anymore. I wouldn't do it over again, but it has been an incredible journey."

What disguised gifts have occurred in your life? What relationships are available as a result?

Aaron loves himself now, which he feels allows him to have compassion for people and really love them.

"The love I was looking for my whole life, I found in me. It is like a spring that comes from within. It's not that I don't need others, I do. It's like being on the airplane, when you are told to put your mask on first and then onto your child. You have to love yourself first before you can love someone else."

A telling story about Aaron was his choice of superhero powers. While his friends chose the ability to fly and the ability to bend bars, Aaron chose the power to heal.

"I wonder how to heal the world of hatred? My wish is that everyone could experience the love I have found. I know we would live longer if we loved ourselves."

How do people feel in your presence? What are you committed to causing for other people?

For Aaron, people are both mirrors and messengers. "People are mirrors, in that I can see myself in them, and they are messengers, in that they give me clues to enjoy life. It is wasteful not to find the joy in life. I wish for all of us to find the good in people."

How others have developed a process to select their relationships:

Steve Knaebel, President of Cummins Mexico

Ed Booth, Steve's close friend, once said with a nostalgic tone and a grin on his face, "The older we get, the more we become like ourselves." As Steve gets older, his relationships become more significant.

Steve makes friends a big priority. Therefore, who he selects as friends is of great importance.

Over the years, Steve has developed a set of values, which he looks for in relationships:

- **Integrity** — the basis for trust, without which relationships cannot flourish or be sustained.

- **Compassion and generosity** — knowing everyone has a bad day or goes through a rough period in their lives, and we all need a sympathetic ear or helping hand.

177

- **Empathy and openness** — builds trust, allows one to learn new ideas and approaches, creates optimism, and is an antidote to boredom.

- **Humility** — without it, one can be closed off from learning, and learning is the key to staying mentally and emotionally alive.

- **Humor** — it's the blood of life and keeps things in perspective; it exposes our shortcomings.

- **Language** — eloquence is entertaining and stimulating, and the precise use of words is key to trust and effective relationships. Knowing a foreign language well is the only way to truly understand the culture in which it is spoken.

- **Worldview** — being interested in how people from countries other than the U.S.A. live and think; accepting their customs and beliefs. Recognizing the creative and energizing benefits of diversity.

- **Environmental stewardship** — respecting, enjoying, and caring about our natural environment.

What process do you utilize to draw relationships into your life? Where do you meet these people?

Steve has found many friends in a variety of non-profit enterprises such as the Peace Corps, Acción International, Special Olympics, EARTH University, and other philanthropic organizations. In these groups, he meets energetic, creative, unselfish, open-minded people who have intellectual curiosity and are going beyond their own needs and desires to help others.

"I am intrigued by others' experiences. They give me a different window on the world, allowing me to see beyond my narrow view. People who have enthusiasm energize me."

How do the people in your life affect you? What do they inspire you to be?

"When I am around some of my friends, it is hard not to be inspired to do more with my life. I think it is vital to take action."

What actions are available for you to take? What would make a difference? How would you affect the world?

Recently, Steve persuaded the chairman of Cummins (a multinational corporation with over twenty-three thousand employees) to use two company jets to take a group of wealthy and influential potential donors from Chicago to Costa Rica's EARTH University.

Many years later, Steve's affect on others was highlighted when he returned to Sao Paulo, Brazil, on business, accompanied by his wife. Upon learning of their visit, almost all the people he had worked with nearly three decades earlier in another company and a nearby city, hosted a traditional Brazilian barbecue for them.

"I had not seen most of them in nearly thirty years, and they all showed up. I realized I made a difference in their lives, and that felt incredible."

How will your friends remember you? What mark do you want to leave on the world?

When Steve dies, he wants to be remembered as a staunchly loyal friend who could be counted on in a pinch. He wants to be someone who made people laugh; created openings for others to realize their potential (including his two sons); stood up for his people and for what was right (even though he knew doing so might possibly set back his career); gave hard-hitting but well-meaning advice; had rock-solid integrity; contributed in some small way to making the world a better place; and "never let his shortcomings keep him from recognizing his failures," as Steve put it, imitating Cantinflas (the famous Mexican actor and comedian).

How can you create relationships that enhance your spark?

From time to time, it is important to look at the people you draw into your life. The people you choose are a mirror and so influential in where you are heading. First, let's perform an exercise to look at who is currently in your life and what role they play:

1) People level assessment – Let's create three categories for the people in your life (keep in mind this is your best assessment and says nothing of these people's capabilities, just where they are currently playing right now):

- People playing a **bigger game** than you in their life – right now in any area important to you (you aspire to be where they currently are)

- People who are **at your level** and succeeding/struggling in the same way you are (you feel at a similar place)

- People who are playing a **smaller game** than you are (they are not at your level, and they may or may not aspire to be)

What do you notice? Which category has the most people in it? Did anyone surprise you? Which category holds your closest friends? Which category holds the people you spend the most time with? Are your best friends the people you spend the most time with?

Do the people in the category above you extend a hand to pull you up to play a bigger game in your life?

Do those below you extend a hand to block you from moving further ahead, or potentially try to pull you down a level where they feel comfortable? How do those below you spend their time?

What do you notice as you think about the people in your life in this way? Please take time to write your answers in your workbook.

When you are ready to play a bigger game, you will draw more people into your life who play on the level above you. This may reduce time with those playing a smaller game, and that is okay. It doesn't mean you don't love them. It just means it is time for you to play a bigger game in life. You can invite anyone to join you.

Do you draw friends, coaches, or colleagues that think BIG? Do they see possibilities and hold space for growth? If you are clear on your purpose, begin to notice kindred spirits with similar visions for their life. You can join forces and propel each other to new heights in your life and make a bigger difference.

2) Purpose and people alignment – Take a moment to ground yourself in your purpose (both your Purposeful Self and your Purposeful Calling). Now let's see how the people in your life line up in connection to your purpose. Again, let's divide everyone into three categories:

- People who **propel you** into your purpose (they enhance your focus; they ask great questions; they support and encourage you; and they value your purpose)

- People who are **neutral** (they neither propel you nor distract you)

- People who **distract you** from your purpose (they actually try to move your focus away from who you want to be and what you want to be about)

How similar are the categories in this list to the list in question 1? How do you feel about the people in each of the categories?

How much of your time do you spend with the people in each category? Are there people missing in your circle? Do you have support gaps?

Does this change how you will look at things moving forward? Please take a moment to write your answers in your workbook.

What do you notice?

3) General people reflection – Let's take a close look at the people you are closest to in life. Answer the following questions with what first comes to mind:

- What qualities do I like most about the people in my life?
- What qualities frustrate me the most with the people in my life?
- Where do people in my life have the best success?
- Where do the people in my life get stuck most often?
- What is the one attitude from Chapter 2 that I wish the closest people in my life held?
- What are the attitudes from Chapter 2 that a majority of the people in my life hold?
- If I could change one thing about someone in my life, what would that be?

As you review your answers above, what do you notice? How do these comments/critiques apply to you?

What one thing do you absolutely *not* want to apply to you?

On a scale of one to ten, with ten being excellent, how would you rate yourself in selecting people in your life?

Please take a moment to write your answers in your workbook.

After reviewing these exercises, how will you approach your current relationships differently? How will you cultivate new relationships going forward?

Powerful grounding questions:
Who could I be that would inspire others? Who could I be that would inspire myself? What is amazing about this person? How does this person affect me?

Signs of excellence:
You will know you are bringing amazing people into your life, when you feel challenged, inspired, and capable.

You will have people who proactively draw you into discussions that cause you to increase your vision.

Your relationships will inspire you to think bigger than you did yesterday. They will raise your consciousness about the choices you make and how those impact your life.

You will see your energy level reaching continuous new highs, and you will be full of the feeling that you can do anything.

You will feel empowered to create the life you have always dreamed of.

Conclusion

I hope you have found access to increasing your spark! Remember, spark is created from who you are *being,* not from what you are *doing.* This is great news, since it allows you to generate spark anyplace and anytime.

When you notice your spark is missing, ask yourself who you are being. How does that reflect your Purposeful Self?

It is important to create discipline in your life so you will notice when your attitudes do not serve you, causing you to stray from your Purposeful Self. Keep your spark present each and every day by creating a personal dashboard—a spreadsheet tracking the ten secrets of spark and measuring how your practice of keeping them alive is going. You may also want to hire a coach to keep you focused on a process to generate your spark. Revisit this book every six months to see if you are keeping spark alive in your life.

No matter where you are or what you are doing, notice what upsets you. Notice which people or events take you away from your best self. This ability to notice will create opportunities for you to take new actions. You will become unstoppable in creating a life you love.

Thank you for joining me on this journey to increase spark in the world. It starts with each of us!

1 - Grateful

Practice by being grateful for each moment that comes your way, no matter what the situation. Notice if you feel you deserve something in life. Continue to distinguish being grateful vs. being entitled to having things go your way.

2 - Freedom

Practice by putting your entire focus on your actions. Take actions consistent with your intentions and completely let go of controlling the results. Trust the results will be a direct reflection of your actions. Notice when you go into controlling mode and what that creates for yourself and others in your life.

3 - Journey Orientation

Practice laughing, loving, and smiling during the day-to-day tasks you perform. Notice if you are enjoying the process of being or if you are more focused on what you are doing and accomplishing. Make yourself a joy to be around and gladly let yourself be interrupted.

4 - Fascination

Practice seeking more from what comes your way. Experience the moment brand new. Resist the urge to know the answer, to look smart. Instead, ask questions about that which you thought you already knew.

5 – At Choice

Practice by selecting the areas in your life where you are stuck or unhappy. Identify the choices that created your situation. Notice if you are blaming anyone or anything for what is going on. Create and act on new choices.

6 – Inclusion

Practice enrolling collaborators, especially those you initially saw as competitors. Resist the urge to claim victory. Take a minute to find a win for all parties. Notice what is created for yourself and others when you are inclusive.

7 – Excellence

Practice showing up for people and your endeavors with the intention of being incredible. Don't sacrifice anything about who you want to be for task perfection.

8 – Humor

Practice finding the humor in a serious situation. See if you can lighten your view during a tense time. If something seems incredibly important to you, notice what place it will have in your life five years from now. Does that open a new possibility for you?

9 – Passion

Practice loving something in every person you greet. Search for what is brilliant about them. Involve all of yourself in your actions. Unleash your passion.

10 - Confidence

Practice taking risks in your dealings with people, in your job, and in your life. Notice what changes. How does confidence affect your spark?